Worlds Apart

A Dialogue of the 1960s

Published by Barfield Press

Books by Owen Barfield:

Poetic Diction: A Study in Meaning
Romanticism Comes of Age
This Ever Diverse Pair
Saving the Appearances: A Study in Idolatry
Worlds Apart: A Dialogue of the 1960's
Unancestral Voice
Speaker's Meaning
What Coleridge Thought
The Rediscovery of Meaning and Other Essays
History, Guilt and Habit
Owen Barfield on C.S. Lewis
Night Operation
Eager Spring
The Rose on the Ash-Heap

Translations:

The Case for Anthroposophy

Forthcoming new editions:

The Silver Trumpet
Orpheus: A Poetic Drama
English People
Short stories
Poetry

www.owenbarfield.org

Owen Barfield

Worlds Apart

A Dialogue of the 1960s

Barfield Press
OXFORD, ENGLAND

Series Editor: Dr. Jane Hipolito

Published by Barfield Press UK, Oxford, England

First published by Faber and Faber, London 1963
Second edition by Wesleyan University Press, Middletown CT 1965
Wesleyan Paperback, 1971
This third edition by Barfield Press, Oxford 2010

A catalogue record for this book is available from
the British Library.

Worlds Apart: A Dialogue of the 1960's by Owen Barfield
ISBN 978-0-9559582-6-7

Printed on paper with Sustainable Forestry Initiative
(SFI) accreditation.

Produced on behalf of
the Owen Barfield Literary Estate.

The Literary Estate promotes and safeguards the works
and intellectual legacy of Arthur Owen Barfield.

D`B

www.owenbarfield.org

CONTENTS

THE PARTICIPANTS

BURGEON (The narrator.) A solicitor with philological interests.

HUNTER A professor of historical theology and ethics.

RANGER A young man employed at a rocket research station.

BRODIE A professor of physical science.

SANDERSON A retired schoolmaster.

UPWATER A biologist engaged on research work.

DUNN A linguistic philosopher.

BURROWS A psychiatrist.

FIRST DAY

IT BEGAN WITH a remark I made to Hunter, when I was visiting him at St. Peter's, where he occupies a Chair in Historical Theology and Ethics. On the way down to Camford I had been reading one of the weeklies—I think it was *The Times Literary Supplement*—and it had left me depressed. What struck me so forcibly, and not for the first time, was that a new book on any subject—history, philosophy, science, religion, or what have you—is always dealt with by a specialist in that subject. This may be fairest from the author's point of view, but it conveys a disagreeable impression of watertight compartments. There were of course plenty of reviews of purely literary productions. Someone had done a definitive edition of Edmund Waller, somebody else had a new angle on Byron and Shelley and their mistresses, and there was the usual crop of dreary-sounding novels. But I found these interested me less than the reviews of books on extra-literary topics, though it was the latter that depressed me so much. The trouble was this. Behind each review there lay a whole network of unspoken assumptions about the nature of life and the universe which were completely incompatible with the corresponding network behind the review on the next page. It was obvious for instance that for both the reviewer and the author of the book on *Psycho-Social History and the Unconscious* everything that both the reviewer and the author (with whom incidentally the reviewer violently disagreed) of the book on *Demythologizing and the Synoptic*

Gospels took for granted was a tissue of exploded fantasy. Again, for the Linguistic Analyst *(Falsification as a Class of Meaning)* and his reviewer all four of these gentlemen must be deemed to be spouting meaningless twaddle. It wasn't that people can think at once confidently and oppositely about almost everything that matters—though that, too, can sometimes be a sobering reflection. It wasn't that they disagreed. I wished they did. What was biting me was the fact that *these minds never met at all.*

'What a lucky chap you are!' I said to Hunter.

We were sitting comfortably together and I had told him what had been passing through my mind.

'How do you mean?'

'To live in a world where contemporary minds really meet. A Senior Common Room that boasts an eminent biologist, a Hebrew scholar, an atomic physicist, two or three philosophers, a professor of comparative religion, a chaplain, a Freudian psychologist, and a leading anthropologist, with Law and English Literature thrown in for good measure, and all dining and wining together nearly every day! What amazingly interesting conversations you must have! What searching private arguments—that best of all kinds of argument, I expect, where the thread is picked up over and over again each time the two disputants meet and the contest goes on for days or even weeks or months on end.'

He smiled—a bit shamefacedly, I thought. 'You've described what it *could* be like,' he said. 'Perhaps it ought to be. But it isn't like that at all. Actually no one ever talks his shop to the other fellow.'

'Do you mean, the watertight compartment business goes on *in the same building!*'

'Yes. If you like to put it that way.'

'In heaven's name *why?*'

'Perhaps it's because the compartments *are* so watertight. From what I know of his books and what he knows of mine, I suppose Mather, for instance, privately regards me as little better than a flat-earther.'

'Exactly. And you probably return the compliment. Yet,' I said, 'you must also regard each other as not wholly lacking in intelligence. Otherwise you would neither of you be where you are.'

There was a pause.

'The French,' I said at last, 'have long used the word "type" in rather a peculiar way—almost as we should say "chap" or "person". It's creeping in here, too—at least I frequently hear my son referring to his friends as "types". Perhaps that's what you do at St. Peter's.'

'Go on.'

'I am suggesting that you mentally classify one another as "types" and leave it at that; so as to avoid—how shall I put it?—so as to avoid *meeting* one another. Except of course for social or administrative purposes.'

'Perhaps there is something in what you say.'

'But then what on earth *do* you talk about—at meals for instance?'

'The news—university appointments—the foibles of our colleagues. Don't worry, Burgeon. Conversation is usually quite brisk.'

Well of course I ought to have felt even more depressed by this reply. But somehow I didn't. Partly because I had been released from envy. I was not, after all, it seemed, shut out from a large freemasonry of discourse where acute minds really met and got down to first principles. Except perhaps for a few undergraduates here and there (who are at the disadvantage of not really *knowing* anything about anything), there was probably no such world. Spiritually we were *all* hermits sitting in our caves, reading *The Times Literary Supplement*, the Sunday papers and so forth—peering through the printed word into one watertight compartment after another—and never seeing a single sluice opened.

Partly, also, because it was then that I had my rash idea.

I shan't easily forget the trouble I had in arranging it. The letters that passed to and fro before I got them all interested and the innumerable further letters and postcards that were exchanged before I found a week-end when they were all free! I have no large and well-staffed country house which I can throw open to my friends as the delightful venue for a symposium. Nor, by an odd coincidence, have they. In the end I secured the use of a cottage in Dorsetshire with a large sitting-room and a garden and enough room for four of us to sleep. And I managed to find hotel beds in the nearest town for the rest. We were to see to our own meals, but were let off mowing the lawn.

Originally there were to be seven of us including Hunter and myself, but at the last moment I suddenly thought it would be a good idea to ask young Ranger to join in. I felt that his fresh and eager optimism might supply an ingredient that would otherwise be rather lacking. He said he would love to come, though he didn't quite see what it was in aid of. He would come straight over from the Rocket Research Station where he worked, but would probably be a bit late.

So it came about that, on a wet Friday night in July, after a good dinner at the largest of the hotels to start us off, we were all sitting together in the sitting-room of the cottage, as I tried rather haltingly to expound, more fully than I had managed in my letters, and on the basis of my old conversation with Hunter, the sort of thing I had in mind. On the whole the response was encouraging: but there was an awkward silence when I finished and switched on the tape-recorder. No one seemed anxious to begin and I realized that I ought to have thought out something definite to lead off with.

Fortunately the silence was broken by the noise of a motor-bicycle and a few minutes later I opened the door to our late arrival, Ranger. He was twenty years younger than any of us. He obviously regarded us with curiosity rather than awe, as he looked about him, but it was a friendly curiosity; and when I had introduced him all round and got him a cup of coffee, he said something about its being very nice of us to invite him to join such a learned gathering.

'That's very polite of you,' I said. 'And that reminds me, I was just saying to our friends before you arrived that, as I see it, politeness is the *only* concession we ought to make to each other in the course of these conversations. No one, I hope, will be personally rude to anyone else, but, subject to that, no holds will be barred. I mean, if A refrains from pressing an argument because he is afraid of hurting B's feelings, undermining his deepest convictions, treading on his dreams, and so forth, the whole thing will be a washout as far as I am concerned.'

I was gratified by a murmured 'Hear hear!'

'By the way, Ranger,' I went on, 'why, after receiving a letter from me in which I set out at great length, and with my customary lucidity, the objects with which we should be meeting this week-end, did you say in your reply that you couldn't quite see what it was all in aid of?'

Ranger hesitated. 'Remember,' I added, 'what I just said about no holds being barred.'

'You mean,' said Ranger, 'you want to know what I really think?'

'I want to know what everyone here really thinks,' I said—and felt rather a prig when I had said it; though it was true. 'Beginning with you, I hope!' I added with a smile.

'It's a bit hard on me,' Ranger began. Then he suddenly collected himself and changed his tone. 'Very well,' he said, 'since you have—very fairly—asked for it—here goes.'

Few, if any, people are capable—at all events in our time—of conversing in the manner which has become traditional in philosophical dialogues from Plato to Brewster and Lowes Dickinson; and not many even of those who can think well and coherently have the faculty of clothing their thoughts *ex tempore* in linked and properly constructed sentences. Chatterboxes apart, I have never in my life heard anyone, who was not actually delivering an address or giving a lecture, continue to speak without pause or interruption for as long as ten minutes. It will be obvious then to the reader that the tape-recording of what passed between us during our (to me) memorable weekend is, in form though not in substance, a very different matter from this book which my friend Owen Barfield, who could not unfortunately be one of us, has kindly composed from it, with such additional help here and there as my memory afforded. Subject to this reservation, I recall that Ranger continued as follows:

RANGER: You see, I have the advantage of knowing something of what is actually going on. I don't know much about the history of science and still less about the history of pre-scientific thought. What I do know is, that three or four hundred years ago for some reason or other the human mind suddenly woke up. I don't know who started it—Bacon, Copernicus, Galileo or someone—and it doesn't seem to me to matter. The point is, that for some reason people began to *look* at the world around them instead of accepting traditional theories, to *explore* the universe instead of just sitting around and thinking about it. First of all they discovered that the earth wasn't flat——

HUNTER: Did they now? Oh well, never mind. Go on.

RANGER: ——and that it was not the centre of the universe, as they had been dreaming, but a rapidly revolving and whirling speck of dust in empty space. Almost overnight about half the ideas men had had about the universe and their own place in it, turned out to be mere illusions. And the other half went the same way, when scientists began applying the new method—practical exploration—to other fields of inquiry—mechanics, chemistry, physiology, biology and, later on, animal and human psychology and so forth. Everything that had been thought before, from the beginnings of civilization down to that moment, became hopelessly out of date and discredited. I suppose it still has an interest for antiquarians and historical specialists and similar types, but apart from that...

Now my difficulty in talking to you people is this. As I understand it, you are going to sit around together and compare certain very different ideas you have about the constitution of the universe, and about man and his place in the universe and about what it is possible to know about man and the universe and all that. Fair enough. But unfortunately at this very moment the new method, the scientific method, the method of actually exploring reality instead of sitting still and talking about it, is in the very act of taking another enormous step forward.

BURGEON: A landing on the moon?

RANGER: Landing on the moon nothing! That will be only a beginning. The point is, that man is on the *move.*

'On the move,' he repeated, 'not on the moon' (and seemed agreeably surprised by his own prowess in epigram), 'out into space—where he has never been before. Who knows

how far he will get? Who knows what altogether new
perspectives will open up when he gets there? All this is
so much more interesting than—well—speculation and
argument.' Ranger paused for a moment and smiled with
a disarming modesty. He went on:

RANGER: Of course, I'm personally concerned with the
development of rocketry and cobblers think there is
nothing like leather. But it's not only *travel* into space.
It's the way all our means of knowing are growing
together. Take radio-astronomy for instance: it had
hardly started at the end of the war. Now there are
about seventy observatories scattered about the
world. We are learning about the radio emission
from the sun and the Milky Way and the extension
of the sun's atmosphere into interplanetary space, we
are beginning to map the distribution of the clouds
of neutral interstellar hydrogen. Already we are
comparing the energy-distribution of cosmic rays as
between one galaxy and another. It's reaching a stage
where we've got the cosmic rays in our pocket; and
once we solve that problem, the nature, the age, and
the origin of the universe—and very likely its
future—will be an open book for science to read.

One just can't *see* ahead. It's too dazzling. New
technical discoveries don't only lead to more new
discoveries—every one of them increases the *rate* at
which discovery proceeds. And that acceleration
increases the rate of acceleration. And I can tell you
it's stepped up pretty high already. I do not see how
this can fail to mean a quite new era in the history of

mankind and I'm afraid I can't help seeing a cosy talk like this with the eyes of the men of two to three hundred years ahead, if they should ever hear of it. Will they find anything we say any more significant (I'm sorry) than *we* find those old arguments the schoolmen used to have about how many angels can stand on the point of a needle or something of that sort?

I looked at Hunter, who does know quite a lot about the history of pre-scientific thought and who thinks the Renaissance was the time when everything went wrong—rather expecting a broadside. But he preferred to maintain a good-humoured silence. He had incidentally dined rather well. Instead, it was Brodie who spoke next.

Brodie is a Scottish Professor of Physical Science, and I was amazed and delighted that I had succeeded in getting him so far south. He is a slow speaker—perhaps a slow thinker—but, if you let him take his time, it's worth it. I had wanted him with us because, besides knowing his technical stuff, he delights to brood in a perplexed sort of way over first principles. At least he likes to talk as though he were perplexed. Actually I think he is less so than he makes out. You could use him very conveniently to demonstrate the etymology of the word *metaphysics*; for he keeps very strictly to pure physics in his lectures, I'm told, reserving for his private hours his acquaintance with the more adventurous speculations of Heisenberg, Schrödinger, Planck and others.

'I'm minding what you said about cobblers, Mr. Ranger,' he began.

'Oh, do drop the "Mr." please, everyone,' I blurted out.

'Very well,' he said, digesting this interruption as carefully as he would have digested some acute observation on the behaviour of anti-particles.

'I thought it was Christian names or nothing with the young people today. I'm minding what you say about cobblers, Ranger. I don't know how it may be with astronomy. I've had to keep my old nose down to physics mostly. If I got your drift rightly, the further you people go with your rockets and satellites and radio-telescopes, the clearer it all grows and the more you feel you know about the universe. So that you can clearly see away on to the time when you'll know everything. I'm just wondering whether it will work out like that at the tail.'

RANGER: No. Of course I don't think we shall ever know everything. There will always be a 'beyond'. But I'm pretty sure we shall know a lot of things we don't know now—and pretty soon, too. Why should there be any doubt about it?

BRODIE: I'm just thinking of what's been going on among the physicists. The old Lord Chief Justice defined a specialist as 'a man who knows more and more about less and less'. But some among us are beginning to wonder if he isn't a man who knows less and less about less and less!

RANGER: Oh yes. I think I know what you mean. You can't make up your minds whether matter consists of waves or particles. And the particles don't behave as you'd expect them to. But surely that's the whole difference between physics and astronomy. Physics

is always going for the smaller and smaller—
molecules—atoms—electrons—nuclei—and so on. But
astronomy and astronautics goes out to the bigger
and bigger. That's why it is such a relief. It's about time
men gave up peering and took to travelling instead.
There's nothing like travel for broadening the mind.
If we do find something quite different from what
we expected, well—all the more interesting!

BRODIE: The question I put is, whether you will find
anything at all!

RANGER: Oh come!

BRODIE: Or put it this way: you might find that your
whole way of thinking about it all has to be abandoned!

RANGER: Yes. And pigs might fly.

'No,' said Brodie slowly, 'it's more possible than that.
You may know that the physicists who are interested in
such things draw a sharp line between what they call
"classical" physics—that is the science of physics as it
was studied before the discovery of relativity and the rest
of it, and modern physics—you can call it "nuclear"
physics if you like. Did you ever hear of Heisenberg?'

RANGER: Of course.

BRODIE: Did you know he said that a constant pursuit of
classical physics *forces a transformation in the very basis
of physics?* What if your astronomy turns out to be
only a classical astronomy?

RANGER: Well?

BRODIE: Then the further you go, the more you'd cut
away the ground from beneath all the ideas that took
you there!

RANGER: In any case, it is only a speculation based on analogy. Why should astronomy be like physics?

HUNTER: I don't think that'll do. There's a good deal more than a mere analogy between astronomy and physics. You said just now, Ranger, that the mind of man woke up for the first time three or four hundred years ago. *If it* did (as to which we'll reserve judgment) the waking began precisely when they started assuming that the laws of physics applied to celestial phenomena. For Aristotle the laws of physics applied only to terrestrial or at most sub-lunary things. What you call 'waking up' began with the substitution of the microscopic for the macroscopic world as the chief object of interest—it began when they started assuming that those laws applied to everything in the universe.

BURGEON: And what about astro-physics?

BRODIE: Exactly. Just how much of your astronomy is based on the spectrum, Ranger? And did you not say that radio-telescopes were just as important as space-travel? How much nuclear physics is there in a radio-telescope—and in what you see through it?

BURGEON: *See!* To my mind the very word 'radio-telescope'—and 'radio-microscope', too, for that matter—is a hidden lie. A *telescope* is an instrument for *seeing* things at a distance. If I understand rightly, you don't *see* anything at all through a radio-telescope except a lot of squiggles on a screen.

RANGER: You're a little out of date. Actually I believe the data are recorded on a punched tape, which is then fed into an electronic computer.

BURGEON: Exactly! You might as well say a man who is looking at a speedometer—no, at a column of figures made up from speedometer-readings, is seeing the speed of the car!

RANGER: Well, isn't he?

BURGEON: He's not looking at it anyway. He's looking at a pointer that measures it.

RANGER: I don't see the difference, as long as they tell him what he wants to know.

HUNTER: I do.

There was a pause. I thought it was about time somebody else joined in, so I turned to Sanderson. Sanderson is a man whom I had included in the party only after considerable hesitation. I do not see him very often and I was not as clear as I should have liked to be about his views. He has tried from time to time to interest me in Goethe's scientific writings. Apart from that, he is a retired schoolmaster of no particular distinction. Like the others, however, he will be speaking for himself; so I need say no more at this stage.

'What do *you* think about the importance of space-travel for the human race?' I asked him.

SANDERSON: I? Well—I'm fascinated by the sheer technical achievement. I always have been fascinated by physical skills—extreme dexterity. Even a circus-rider standing upright on a galloping horse gives me a catch in the throat; even if the whole show is rather silly... there is something awfully moving about *deftness*, when it's carried to a high pitch. Who was that clown who was such a marvellous juggler?

Grock. You looked on for a bit, and you suddenly heard yourself whispering: 'Oh, you *beauty!*' with your eyes growing wet. But I confess the amount of human *thinking* that has gone into all these gadgets—including the gadgets they use for making the gadgets—electronic computers and so forth—frightens me rather.

BURGEON: Yes. But the question is, do you feel that space-travel is important for the human race—and in particular for its prospects of extending our knowledge of the universe?

SANDERSON: Do I think space-travel is likely to be an important turning-point in the evolution of mankind? I suppose the answer to that is no. I can't get very excited about the prospect of man getting farther and farther into space.

RANGER: Why not?

SANDERSON: Because I think he is there already.

'And what may that mean?' said Hunter rather sharply. Sanderson did not reply for a moment. Then he said: 'I am inclined to think it was a needlessly provocative remark and I apologize for it. You had better leave me out. Can we go on from where we were, Burgeon?'

'Perhaps,' I said to Hunter, 'you will try and explain to Ranger here the difference between seeing a speedometer and seeing speed.'

HUNTER: I don't think I will, though. You know. Burgeon, all this is a very good illustration for me of what you said about watertight compartments. I believe it's what led up to this symposium?

He looked round at the others, and most of them
nodded. They had heard quite a lot from me about
watertight compartments.

HUNTER: Three people talk about the possibilities of
space-travel and I listen. But I can't *join* in this
discourse; I can't even be really interested in it—
because everything they feel and say is based on
assumptions which are never discussed between them,
since they are taken for granted by all of them—and
never discussed with people like me, who don't
share them, because—well, because of the watertight
compartments! Ranger spoke of the human mind
'waking up'—what he meant, of course, was the
beginnings of modern natural science. Whether you
agree with him or not that there was never any other
natural science, or that space-travel is the next step in
it, you all seem to take it absolutely for granted that
modern science is in some way relevant to the *dignity*
of man; that it has a high human value—and very
likely the highest. And nearly everyone today starts
from the same assumption. I not only disagree with
that assumption; I regard it as dangerous nonsense.
Don't misunderstand me. I'm not attacking science,
though I know I shall be accused of doing so,
whatever I say. Every kind of knowledge, including
science, is valuable. But all kinds of knowledge are
not valuable in the same way, or for the same
reason. There are many different kinds of knowledge,
and one kind is the kind which we require to enable
us to control our material environment and make

it serve our purposes. You can call it knowledge about *things* if you like. But there is also another kind of knowledge—knowledge about *man* and about the values which make him man and the best way of preserving them; knowledge about his relation to God and God's creatures. The mistake you make—the mistake nearly everyone makes—is to assume that the first kind necessarily includes the second.

Perhaps this is because in the old days it often did. As long as men wanted to be wise and not simply 'knowing', they assumed that you could not learn anything about nature (except for purely utilitarian purposes) without at the same time learning something about man and the God who created and sustains them both. This is where modern science came in. Its whole basis—the very thing that was new about it—was the assumption that, if you want to know about *things*, you must assume that they are *merely* things. You must treat them as objects for the senses, but as independent in all other respects of man and his spirit and his values. And *a fortiori* you must leave out God. Moreover, if you want to know about nature, you must treat *her* as a collection of things in precisely that sense. If you want to know about the bodies of animals and men, you must treat them as things—as a surgeon does, for instance. I do not criticize them for that in the least. I applaud them for it. It is almost certainly the right way of going about it. But they are too stupid—or too clever—to know when to stop. They go on trying to extend the same method into a territory where it is *ex hypothesi* inapplicable—the human soul, for instance—or the human psyche, if you prefer it. With the result that they contort themselves in a frenzied attempt to treat *that* as a thing too. On their own showing, the *thing* is a *not-psyche* and the *psyche* is a *not-thing*. But they fancy that, if you turn round quickly enough, you will see the back of your head in the mirror.

The other thing I criticize in modern science—or in the enthusiasts for science—is this. They have got hold of this method of knowledge, which by definition, excludes man and all his values from the object to be known and they have found it very useful. But not content with this, they go on insisting that the method itself has a *human* value and enhances *human* dignity. They are like children thinking they can have it both ways. First they insist on cutting out awe and reverence and wisdom and substituting sophistication as the goal of knowledge; and then they talk about this method of theirs with reverence and awe and expect us to look up to them as wise and venerable men.

It was Dunn, the analytical philosopher or linguistic analyst, or whatever I ought to call him, who broke the silence.

'I didn't hear Ranger say anything about awe and reverence,' he said. 'I am obliged to Hunter for another illustration of this watertight compartment business! I can't say I *differ* from him. I never got so far as that. I listened without participating at any single point in any single thing he was saying. I wouldn't actually use the word "nonsense", if he hadn't done so himself. But as he did, I will be frank and say that it had almost the effect of nonsense on me.'

BURGEON: I wonder why. I thought he was rather good.

DUNN: Because it was based from beginning to end on one of those unshared assumptions you were talking about. Namely, it assumes a duality of body and mind which has been hopelessly discredited in my view both physiologically and, at least since Wittgenstein, philosophically.

RANGER: I knew there was some catch, though I couldn't lay my finger on it.

At this point Upwater, the biologist among us, put in a word. 'I listened very carefully,' he said, 'and I think I agree broadly with Hunter's conclusions—though of course I have nothing in common with the dualism—and indeed supernaturalism—on which he bases them. For a long time now we have been too much concerned with the "conquest" as we call it, of external nature. We have forgotten that nature is neither our enemy nor our servant. We have forgotten that we ourselves *are* nature and what is more we are its growing point.'

HUNTER: That cock won't fight. The whole edifice of modern science, including the theory of evolution, is based on that very dualism. Abandon that and you abandon the whole scientific method, lock, stock and barrel. Incidentally you abandon consciousness itself— but we'll leave that out for the moment.

RANGER: I don't see why. Once you have discovered that what we used to call the mind is really the same thing as the brain, it seems to me to follow that the only way to examine the mind is to experiment with the brain. Isn't that just what the experimental psychologists are doing?

HUNTER: I wasn't talking about the mind you think you are examining, I was talking about the mind that is *doing* the examining.

RANGER: Well, it's only another mind. Someone else can examine that in the same way, I suppose.

Hunter sighed in a resigned sort of way and was gathering himself for a reply, when I cut in.

'Do you mind, Hunter?' I said. 'Can we leave it for a bit? I would very much like to go a little further, first, with Brodie's thing about classical physics and the relation between physics and astronomy. Unless,' I added anxiously, 'anybody would first like to explain why all *that* was nonsense?'

BRODIE: As a matter of fact, just this problem of the duality between matter and mind—and I mean the observing mind—the duality between subject and object—is the thing that's bothering us most at the moment. When I say 'us', you'll understand I mean a few philosophical physicists and a few innocent bodies like myself, who try to keep up with them without a great deal of success. Einstein's Relativity, Planck's Constant, Bohr's Principle of Complementarity are all——

BURGEON: Wait a minute, Brodie. You're going too fast for some of us. You forget I'm no more than a simple lawyer with a bit of a taste for philology. What do I know about Planck and Bohr? First of all, what do you mean by 'classical' physics?

BRODIE: I thought you'd all know that. Roughly we mean the general system of theories about the nature of the universe, which is based on the discoveries made between Galileo and Newton and which treats these not as working hypotheses but as a true description of the world.

HUNTER: Could the system as a whole be characterized as the theory that the universe is constructed out of an infinite number of minute particles, each of which is indivisible and indestructible, and each of which acts on the other and is acted on by them in accordance with mechanical laws?

BRODIE: That would do pretty well. First it was atoms, then electrons and then other particles too. The ultimate particles grew smaller and smaller. Originally the atom was supposed to be an indivisible whole. (Isn't that what the word *atom* means, Burgeon?) Perhaps the theory was already doomed as soon as it was discovered that the atom itself was made up of parts, like everything else. But they went on taking it for granted for a long time—and indeed some still do.

SANDERSON: Just as *we* go on taking it for granted, you might have added (for that was the point we started from), that the astronomical discoveries from Galileo to Newton are true descriptions of the universe outside the earth.

BRODIE: In that case I don't know that there has been anything so far to suggest that we are far wrong. All I said was that I shouldn't be surprised if we *did* soon come up against something.

After a slight pause Ranger spoke. 'You haven't mentioned the Quantum Theory,' he said to Brodie, 'and wave mechanics. Isn't classical physics called "classical" mainly because it hadn't yet discovered them?'

BRODIE: I haven't mentioned them, because I don't think I'm called on to give a lecture on the history of physical science—or of anything else for that matter. I doubt these technicalities are much to our purpose here. What *may* be material is the fact, now accepted almost everywhere, that the ultimate particle—or whatever we ought to call it—the ultimate object of observation—is not in fact independent of the observer—though the whole method of physical science is based on the assumption that it is.

HUNTER: Is it the *existence* or the *behaviour* of the ultimate particle that is dependent on the observer?

BRODIE: Certainly its behaviour. As to its existence, I don't know and perhaps no one does. Anyway, the interdependence is something which classical physics could never have dreamed of admitting. And I believe it's there you have the fundamental difference between classical physics and modern physics.

HUNTER: 'The transformation in the very basis', in fact?

BRODIE: It looks like it.

'Before we leave this line,' I said, looking at the two members of the party who had not yet opened their mouths, 'there is something I have never been able to understand about even classical physics, let alone modern. May I raise it now?' There was a general assent, so I continued.

BURGEON: *My* question is, what is the relation between this mysterious world of whirling particles with vast empty spaces between them that the physicists talk about and the actual world we live in—flowers, horses, clouds, sounds, scents and so forth?

RANGER: I don't follow. It *is* the actual world.

HUNTER: It obviously *isn't.* I never saw a particle in my life, but I see and hear all the things Burgeon mentioned quite clearly every day.

RANGER: That's simply because your only contact with it is through your senses.

DUNN: I don't agree with that way of putting it. As far as I'm concerned, I don't perceive 'through' anything. I just perceive.

BURGEON: Yes. I know that's the usual answer, Ranger. But if the real world is *not* something we perceive with our senses, but only something we *infer* from what we perceive, then dash it—what is all the fuss over science *about?* You said just now that three or four hundred years ago the human mind suddenly woke up and began to *look* at the world instead of theorizing about it!

RANGER: Yes. And so it did. Surely that's the whole difference between us and the Middle Ages! We've learned to use our eyes.

Brodie grinned a little. 'Be careful, Ranger,' he said. 'I think I'm with you on the whole. But Burgeon has really got something there.'

HUNTER: Did you ever see Shaw's *Saint Joan*? Do you
remember the curtain line to Act II? The Bishop has
just told Lahire that Copernicus was 'the sage who
held that the earth goes round the sun', and Lahire's
comment is: 'What a fool! *Couldn't he use his eyes?*'
RANGER: I don't see what you're driving at.

'I do,' said Brodie. 'I wonder,' he added slowly, and
began feeling in his pockets, 'if any of you gentlemen ever
looked at Galileo's *Dialogue of Two World Systems?* For my
sins, I once did. It's an awful long-winded affair. If you
look carefully, you'll find some queer contradictions in it.
There are two passages I made a special note of. If
anyone would like to hear them, I have them with me.
I just thought they might crop up, you see. In one place,'
he added, uncrumpling the bit of paper he had succeeded
in finding, the great man lays it down that: *In every
hypothesis of reason, error may lurk unnoticed, but a discovery
of sense cannot be at odds with the truth.*' He looked up.
'Well—that's plain-spoken enough,' he said.

'Yes,' said Ranger. 'It's obvious to us, of course. But I
suppose it's obvious partly because he saw it first and put
it so clearly.'

'Very clearly indeed,' said Brodie. 'You'll hardly believe,
though, that about fifty pages farther on the same man
writes in the same book.... I'll read it:

'*I cannot sufficiently admire the eminence of those men's
wits, that have received and hold it* [he's talking of the
Copernican theory] *to be true, and with the sprightliness of
their judgments offered such violence to their own senses, as
that they have been able to prefer that which their reason*

dictated to them, to that which sensible experiments represented
most manifestly to the contrary.

'There's some more that I won't read—but this is how
he rounds it off:

'*I cannot find any bounds for my admiration, how that*
reason was able in Aristarchus and Copernicus, to commit
such a rape on the senses, as in despite thereof to make herself
mistress of their credulity.'

'In other words,' said Hunter, after a slight pause,
'which of them *really* relies more on sense-perceptions—
Aristotelian science or modern science? By Jove, what if
it's all been a gigantic hoax? Look here, Ranger, how
much of that stuff you were rubbing in about radio-
astronomy and clouds of interstellar hydrogen and so
forth is *actually* what Galileo called "a discovery of sense"
and how much of it is thought-spinning? I conceded that
a knowledge of *things* is valuable in its own way. But
have you even got *that?* Haven't you got simply a huge
inverted pyramid of ideas—mathematics if you like—
erected on a tiny apex of ascertained facts? An apex that
is getting smaller and smaller every day? More and more
piled on less and less?'

RANGER: What we have got *works*. That's the point.
We can predict events accurately and apply our
predictions technologically.

SANDERSON: We grant that. But how much of what is
called science *is* technological? How much of it is
verifiable even to that extent? It doesn't apply, for
instance, to anything in the past—archaeology,
palaeontology, about half of anthropology, the

history of the earth, the age and dimensions of the universe, and so forth—or to anything very remote in space, such as the physical constitution of the stars concluded from astro-physics. There is a whole vast realm of science—perhaps the major part of it— where it has nothing *but* the inverted pyramid.

RANGER: I'm afraid you're taking me out of my depth.

I had been feeling for some little while that it was about time someone else took a hand, and I turned at this point to Upwater. Upwater, as I have mentioned, is a biologist. He has a good research appointment somewhere or other—I forget whether it is academic or industrial. It will be enough, I think, if I say that I had invited him because he is a sort of biological Brodie. That is to say, he is technically trained and his bread and butter depends on his professional activities, which are exacting enough. At the same time he keeps alive a certain speculative interest in the wider implications of his field and is not too austerely contemptuous of all attempts to explain to the public outside what is going on in the laboratories. If a book by Sir Julian Huxley—or even Teilhard de Chardin— appears and is talked about, he will at least look at it, though it is difficult to get him to express any opinion of his own on the sort of general conclusions they draw. I had hoped—and the event showed that I was justified— that he himself might be 'drawn' a little farther than usual on this occasion. For he knew in advance that it would be mainly the general implications of his stuff in which the symposium would be interested.

'What *you* think about all this?' I asked him.

UPWATER: I don't know if my particular compartment is quite watertight; I hope not. But let us try and see.

What has struck me most while I have been listening is, that you have all been talking all the time about two things: first, about space—what may be found and what happens in it, whether on a large or a small scale; and secondly about some big change that took place in the mind of man three or four hundred years ago.

I agree that the scientific revolution was a very important step in the evolution of humanity—which I take to be the gradual realization by man of the potentialities implanted in him by nature or, if you like, of the potentialities latent in nature itself. It's the same thing; for man's *knowledge* of nature is obviously the latest stage of that evolution—the stage we are now in. I agree also with Ranger about the startling increase in the rate of acceleration. But I think he overestimates the importance of exploring space—outwards—and probably Brodie exaggerates the importance of exploring it inwards (if that is the right word; it seems to me to be one way of describing what physical science tries to do). I am not all that interested in space. After all, it was not only the frontiers of space that the human mind broke through as the result of the scientific revolution. We have achieved an entirely new perspective of *time* also—and we have achieved that much more recently. Only since Darwin, in fact.

But we *have* done it, and the new knowledge we have won with the discovery of evolution simply alters everything—including our scale of values: including our appraisal of history. In the perspective habitual to me this change in our way of thinking that took place three or four hundred years ago sometimes looks pretty negligible. We biologists think in millions of years rather than hundreds.

I suppose a good deal depends on what you mean when you use the word 'man'. You have been talking of him as if he were a fixed quantity—something which has always been the same as it is now and always will be. Now when I think of man, I think of him as a developing primate; an organism with millions of years of evolution behind him and, in all probability, at least as many millions in front of him. To philosophize about man as he happens to be in the twentieth century is like—well, it's as if a botanist who had never seen a root or a flower, were to take a thin cross-section of a tree-trunk and think that, by examining that, he could find out what a tree is and how it is related to the earth and the surrounding air.

Of course his contemporary adventures in space— or with his radio-microscope—are all a part of the vast process, and may prove to be an influential part. But much more important than any knowledge of nature, or of himself, that he can gain in that snapshot way is his new knowledge of nature (and of himself as a part of nature) as an *evolving* process and of all the rich possibilities of mutation inherent in the laws governing his heredity. Especially if, as now seems probable, he gains enough knowledge of those laws to enable him to work with them, so as to control, perhaps to create, his own future development. That is why the work of Crick and Watson, for instance, at Cambridge on the nucleic acids seems to me infinitely more important and more interesting than anything that is happening in nuclear physics or radio-astronomy, or the development of space-travel.

'H'm,' said Hunter, after a short pause, 'on and on and on and up and up and up! *Sub specie scalae mobilis.*'

'Meaning?' asked Ranger.

'The universe as moving staircase.'

Upwater was unperturbed. 'I think I know what you mean,' he said patiently. 'The reaction against nineteenth-century ideas of evolution was not unjustified. It would have come, I think, on purely scientific grounds even if their optimistic ideas of inevitable human progress had not been hit by human behaviour in the last thirty years, as they have been. Although they spoke so confidently, the nineteenth-century biologists and zoologists really knew very little about the actual mechanism of heredity and the Darwinian theory of progress by natural selection was coming under fire before the Communists and the Nazis came on the scene,

'But really, you know, all that reaction is itself rather out of date by now. On the other hand, the rediscovery of Mendel and the enormous advance in genetical theory has established the Darwinian theory beyond all doubt as the cause of biological evolution. But on the other hand we no longer think of *future* evolution as likely to be biological in the old sense.'

HUNTER: That seems to me to be another way of saying that you think evolution has *stopped*. If you are not talking biology, you may use the *word* 'evolution' but you are simply using it as a metaphor.

UPWATER: Oh no. Evolution must be taken to cover all the processes of change and development in the universe. Inorganic evolution was going on for billions of years before organic or biological evolution began with the appearance of the first living organism—the first object to have acquired the capacity of reproducing itself. But it is advanced by different causes at different stages of itself. Inorganic evolution had to rely on mechanical causes; but as soon as life appears, the principles of self-reproduction and variation which it introduces bring with them the new factor of natural selection. Moreover that was not the last major advance, as the nineteenth-century evolutionists appeared to think.

With the appearance of consciousness, and a little later (for it *is* a little in terms of the whole vast process) with the growth of *mind* in *homo sapiens* an entirely new phase of evolution set in, bringing with it a new cause or method of change. Through the human properties of speech and conceptual thought the cosmic process began to reflect itself in a microcosm. At the same time, with the coming of the new technique of *communication*, which language—and later of course writing and printing—brought with it—the importance of purely biological evolution began to fade. For the third phase, the phase of psycho-social evolution, as it has been well called, had already arisen to take its place.

Very little work has yet been done on this, though some anthropologists have made a good beginning. You see, mind is also self-reproducing—only in this case we use the word 'tradition'. And for this reason there is a cultural as well as a biological heredity and we have now to study, not only the evolution of biological organisms, but also that of cultures and civilizations—and even of ideas themselves. It is only in this way that we can learn about the last bit of the past, and about the whole of future evolution.

All this has its bearing on my reaction to your argument, to *any* argument, on the relation between mind and matter. In a sense I do feel it to be nonsense. The unitary view is so much simpler. Because, where there is no distinction, there is no relation to worry about. For me reality is a process, and that process is evolution, and it includes us. You can call it 'nature' if you like. It makes no difference. We are the part of it that has become self-conscious. The mindless universe did not split into two universes because it generated mind, any more than the inorganic universe changed from one to two, because it generated living organisms. It is true, I have heard it argued that this view implies a kind of latency, or potentiality, of life and even of mind, in the inorganic world from the start. But I doubt that. In any case the point is, that since the evolution of consciousness, certain combinations of the world-stuff *have* acquired recognizable mental attributes.

It is obvious to me that these mental attributes are themselves the instrument of further evolution, and that that is their true importance. But that does not mean that I think of progress or evolution as a moving staircase. On the contrary. For, in the third phase of evolution—the psycho-social phase in which we live— and with the development of conceptual thought— another new factor, another method of change made its appearance. The element of *intention*, based on the faculty of choosing between alternatives. The human mind does not only *reflect* the macrocosm in its systems of ideas, it gives to it its whole significance, since it is only in the human mind that the process, which is reality, becomes self-conscious. It follows that, through its spearhead or growing-point of the human mind, the universe may in future influence, or perhaps—who knows?—conduct, its own evolution.

Personally I find the thought an inspiring one, and I don't mind saying—but perhaps I have been going on too long?

We shook our heads.

UPWATER: Then I would just like to add this. When I speak of man—or the world through man—influencing or guiding its own evolution, I am not only thinking of our new knowledge of genetics and the new technique to which it may give rise, though that may well be an important factor. We may well find ourselves able to make conscious use of the biological processes of heredity which have hitherto operated at random. It may be we ourselves and not natural selection, who will determine what mutations are brought about—just as socially organized man already takes a part in deciding which shall survive. It is impossible to say what sort of altogether new man we might learn to produce in that way.

HUNTER: You will produce the kind *you want* to produce—the kind of human being which *you*, in your wisdom, decide is the right kind. And God help him!

UPWATER: As far above and beyond man, as we know him, perhaps, as man has risen above the dumb animals. Indeed the production of such a new species may well be the next step for which evolution is even now gathering its forces.

But it was not so much all this that I had in mind. I said that, with the development of conceptual thought, the new elements of *intention* and *choice* appeared. But that was not the only new thing. You see, biological evolution works mainly in the increase of variation. Simple organisms become more and more complex, and at the same time the number of different species multiplies. The whole world of nature grows more and more varied, more and more complex, more and more multiplex. But with the appearance of consciousness, and above all of human language and thought, a new *principle* of evolution appeared. It was not only the springboard for a new leap forward; from one point of view it was the start of something like a change of *direction*—in a way a *reversal* of direction. Thought is self-reproducing, as

I said; but it is also (in the form of tradition and culture) self-maintaining. Above all, however— and this distinguishes it from all that went before—it is interpenetrating. Its characteristic tendency is towards unity, whereas the characteristic tendency of biological nature is towards variety. Henceforth, alongside the phenomenon of variation, and perhaps gradually superseding it, you have the phenomenon of—what? I suppose *convergence* is the best term for it.

No. I am spoiling it by overstatement. I said 'new'; but I should only have said: new on the almost planetary level, which it is now attaining. The principle of convergence *was* of course operative in the earlier stages of evolution as well as that of variation. Atoms associated to produce molecules and molecules to produce cells. Cells, besides proliferating, converged in those patterned processes we call living organisms.

In primitive peoples, tribal customs, ethical systems, languages themselves, are innumerable. I forget how many Bantu languages there are; but I believe it runs into four figures. But as civilization— which is the name for the latest phase of evolution— the convergent phase—progresses, this variety does not increase. On the contrary, it diminishes. Tribal customs become articulate in complicated polytheisms; the polytheisms syncrete with one another, as communication between the tribes develops and increases; languages become national in their scope instead of merely tribal; the syncreted polytheisms converge into monotheism and monotheism in its turn into that abstract principle of the uniformity of nature, which underlies all science.

Human beings are already too complex and highly organized to associate by chemical combination in the manner of cells. But they do combine in cultural and social organisms. Thinking, then, is the process of convergence operating in human beings to form something analogous to a new single organism of global dimensions; and I take it that this was what Teilhard de Chardin meant, when he said 'Reflection planetizes.'

It is this process, which we as the servants of evolution, are, at this point in evolution, called upon to further, if we can. At least that is how I see it. And it needs some furthering. I painted a rosy picture of successful convergence just now. But it is only half the picture, if that. I suspect that future historians will depict our age as one in which convergence had hardly begun. For so many of the primitive stages remain, so much of the biologically produced variety is still untranscended. The tribal customs still survive in many parts of the world, and so does polytheism. There is even more than one monotheism—which is a kind of logical absurdity. Evolution produces, among other things, diseases which obstruct and impede its own progress and the major disease of our time is the absence of any common frame of reference, of any general agreement about the nature of man, his place in the universe and his destiny. It has its geo-political

aspect, too. There is the huge split between the
ideologies of the Eastern and the Western halves of
the earth. The East has its own way of imposing
unity. And here in the West—where the scientific
view is supposed to be generally accepted—what
do we see? Instead of local convergence, increasing
fragmentation. Mental nature, operating through
individual intelligences, keeps on producing obstacles
to its own process, new variations which obstruct the
process and might even end by damming it up
altogether, if they are not grasped and dealt with.

How many varieties, even here in the West—and
conflicting varieties too—there are in man's view
of nature, or in the view which nature, through
the human brain, takes of herself! Supernaturalists,
behaviourists, psycho-analysts, naturalists, tech-
nologists, rub shoulders with one another and that
is about all they do rub. Burgeon's 'watertight
compartments' in fact! It's true. Opportunities for
interpenetration have never been greater—and yet
our minds are worlds apart. This is the way I see it
and—you may smile—but it was for this reason, as
at least one tiny step in convergent evolution, that I
welcomed the idea of this symposium when Burgeon
put it to me—and that I am glad to take part in it.

Hunter looked round to see if anyone else was ready to
say anything, but we all wanted a little more time than he
did to arrange our thoughts; and he began:

'It seems to me, Upwater, that you have been talking
about two distinct processes, which have very little to do

with each other; and I don't see what justification you have for lumping them both together as one single process, just because one followed the other in time. The first was the process of biological evolution, with which we are all familiar enough. The second seemed to me to be simply what we used to call *history* —partly actual and partly prophesied. What is gained by stuffing the two into the same bag and calling it "evolution", which I should have thought was a vague and wide enough term already? Evolution is, by definition, an unconscious process — something, to put it colloquially, which "goes on of its own accord" as nature herself does. "Planned evolution" is therefore a contradiction in terms.'

BURGEON: But why shouldn't it change its definition, as other words have done?

UPWATER: H'm! I have a feeling that the record is not quite straight here. Give a dog a bad name and hang him! A little while ago you were disparaging evolution because it was like a moving staircase. Now, when it is suggested that it includes human vohtion and human effort, you say it is not evolution!

HUNTER: *Touche!* Perhaps there is more in this meeting notion of yours than I thought, Burgeon!

UPWATER: I cannot see the difficulty. Since consciousness, and with it thinking and planning, have themselves evolved into existence, why are they and their working-out not to be regarded as a part of evolution? You might as well say that, because animals, when they appeared, began eating vegetables and preying on each other, they were somehow outside the evolutionary process which produced the plants and the other animals they destroyed.

HUNTER: It's no use. I withdraw my argument from definition; but it just won't do. You cannot treat thinking as a stage in evolution without cutting away the ground from beneath everything you say—including *that* thing. Either Reason is outside the natural process or we might as well stop talking and play Puss-in-the-corner instead!

RANGER: But *why?*

HUNTER: Can't you see? Upwater is *now* saying that all the words he spoke to us before were part of the natural process—just as everything everybody else says must be. But he didn't believe that, while he was actually speaking them. While he was actually speaking so eloquently (and I mean that), he assumed, as we all do, that they were something quite different. He assumed that they were *true*—and that if some other part of the process gets up and says the opposite, that opposite also is not simply a manifestation of natural forces, but is what we call *error.*

RANGER: Why shouldn't it be both?

HUNTER: Oh dear! I've been through this so often... especially with pupils. Look here, Ranger, everyone who thinks it worth while arguing believes in the validity of rational thought; for he believes that *his* thought at least is independent of irrational causes. And everyone who is convinced by an argument, believes that the other fellow's thought is independent in the same way. Perhaps I ought to try and make it clearer. What is the difference between a rational cause and an irrational one? X thinks there is a man hiding behind the curtain on the wall. We may know that he thinks that *because* he saw a man slip behind it an hour ago, has been watching the curtain ever since and has seen no one come away from it. Alternatively we may know that he thinks that *because* he is suffering from paranoia, as a result of which he is convinced that most of his friends, the police, the judiciary and the government are in a conspiracy to destroy him. In the first case we attend to and may be convinced by what he says. In the second we don't because we know his thought is due to an irrational (because a pathological) cause. Namely paranoia. In both cases we know *why* he thinks as he does; in both cases we know the *cause* of his thought. But in the first case the cause is a rational one, precisely because it is *not* what the second one is—a part of the natural process.

DUNN: Well—*really*!

BURGEON: What is the matter?

DUNN: Only that Hunter seems to be genuinely unaware of the fact that he has been using the term 'irrational' in two quite different senses. We say a stone is 'irrational', meaning that it has *no* reasoning faculty. When we say a man is irrational, we mean that his reasoning faculty is *disordered*. Of course we distrust the conclusions of a disordered brain; but how does that prove that we ought to distrust those of a normal one?

HUNTER: I think I must admit to some equivocation. Perhaps it wasn't a very good example. But it doesn't affect the principle. What I was trying to illustrate was that, if the conclusion of an argument is to be true, all the steps must be related as grounds and consequents. But natural (that is, non-rational) events are related only as causes and effects; and there is no connection between the two different kinds of connection.

BURGEON: I wonder whether we are getting at the true distinction—though the words are loosely used as synonyms—between the *cause* why, and the *reason* why.

HUNTER: The point is, that everyone, while he himself is arguing, assumes that the reason why he himself thinks what he is at the moment expressing is of the first kind. He knows that, as soon as it is shown to be the second kind, namely a natural cause, the thought which this cause made him think will be automatically invalidated. Now it is absurd to apply this test to every particular thought and not to all thoughts taken collectively. If any one thought is invalidated by being shown to be the product of natural causes, it follows that the whole concatenation of human thought—I call it Reason, but the name doesn't matter—is invalidated if it, too, is the product of natural causes. Those causes being assumed, as Upwater and you assume them, to be irrational. And it's no use your saying: 'Why shouldn't it be both?' If you assume that there is such a thing as truth and error at all, then you assume that *some part* of the thinking process is not a product of irrational causes. I don't in the least mind how much of the thought-process you assign to nature. Once you concede that some part of it is outside, it is only that part I am talking about.

It was Upwater's turn to sigh. 'Yes,' he said, 'I know there are certain purely logical difficulties. And I perceive the old supernaturalism intends to go down fighting. It's a pity, because I am convinced that all hope of any further progress depends on our superseding it.'

HUNTER: And you yourself will be fighting for it every time you talk sense—as you so often do! I have been trying to show you that you yourself are a supernaturalist—in the sense in which you are using the word—because you always do in practice assume that there is something other than the total process of irrational nature, and that we participate in that other every time we think a valid thought.

So does Ranger and so does everyone else here—otherwise they would not *be* here. Ranger put up that picture of a series of brains examining each other. Can you *really* not see what I mean? You may go on gabbling—sorry, *using*—words like supernaturalism, dualism, psycho-somatic (and I have no quarrel with that word, properly used), input, feed-back, output and the rest of it, till you are black in the face. You may, for all I know, succeed in detecting a physical or electrical change in the brain for the airiest fragment of a frolic of a half-thought thought that ever hovered for an instant in the fancy of Mercutio. But you can never, without talking nonsense, obliterate the ultimate cleavage between (*a*) consciousness itself and (*b*) that *of which* it is conscious.

RANGER: I'm afraid I *still* don't quite see why.

HUNTER: Because by the very act of denying it you affirm it. Because by denying anything at all, you affirm that such a thing as 'denial' is possible. Because by affirming the possibility of denial you affirm that a *that-which-is-conscious-of* can pass judgment on a *that-of-which-it-is-conscious*. And in doing so you re-affirm the very detachment of subject from object which you are pretending to deny. Your denial is like a sentence consisting of the words 'This is not a sentence.' It's as if a man were to open his mouth and say: 'I am not speaking.'

And having said all that, I've done no more than say over again that that cleavage is the immediate experience on which all mental experience is founded. I'm sorry to have been so long-winded. The obvious is the hardest thing of all to point out to anyone who has genuinely lost sight of it.

DUNN: There is a good deal I could say to that. I'll say it now, if you like, Burgeon. But I fear it would only spoil the fun and perhaps you would rather I deferred it.

BURGEON: I don't think you need fear, in present company, that anyone will take silence as implying assent. Ask Burrows here, who has hardly said a word so far!

RANGER: It all sounds rather fine-drawn to me. I suppose it's philosophy.

DUNN: That's just what it is.

RANGER: How does it apply to the general picture of evolution we had from Upwater?

HUNTER: Well, for instance—but haven't you chaps had enough? I shall only be saying it all over again.

BURGEON: I think you should go on a little.

HUNTER: Very well then—Upwater said, among other things, that the theory of natural selection is now definitely established. Was Upwater's mouth opening and shutting, and noises coming out of it, simply part of the process of evolution of irrational nature or did he mean that what he said was *true?*

RANGER: I begin to see what you are driving at.

HUNTER: Down to a hundred or so years ago, lots of other men used to open their mouths and send noises out of them. And those noises seemed to mean exactly the opposite. Instead of saying that man has risen slowly from a worse state to his present better state, they said that he had fallen from a better state—Paradise or the Golden Age or the like—to his present worse state. If both sets of noises are simply natural processes, why should we believe the second and not the first? Why should we believe either of them when, by explaining them away as the result of irrational causes, we have ruled out their whole relevance to truth and falsity?

It was Upwater who answered this time, and there was a hint of distaste in his voice. 'You want to make everything so absolute,' he said. 'Of course, in a sense, scientific theories are never *final*. They approximate more and more to the truth. That is why science is, in my view, a method of knowledge in accord with evolution. Whereas the older methods were not.'

HUNTER: So that, when you said that the theory of natural selection is now definitely established, you meant that it is definitely proved to be true and may turn out to be false?

UPWATER: I would rather say 'not so true as we thought'. Yes, I suppose that is about what we mean by a scientific hypothesis.

SANDERSON: It's not what I mean by it.

BRODIE: Nor what I mean.

BURGEON: What about you. Ranger?

RANGER: It sounds all right to me.

BURGEON: Dunn?

DUNN: I disagree with Upwater's definition of a scientific hypothesis; but not for the reasons given by Hunter.

BURGEON: And you, Burrows?

BURROWS: For me the question whether a statement is true or not cannot be answered without a full knowledge of the speaker and his state of mind at the time.

HUNTER: Let's just get this quite clear, Upwater. You are quite sure, I gather, that the theory of natural selection can never be proved *wholly* untrue—less true, for instance, than the account of creation given in *Genesis?*

UPWATER: Quite sure.

HUNTER: Then there is some part of the theory that *has* definitely been proved to be true, even if we don't yet know which part?

UPWATER: Certainly.

HUNTER: By revelation?

UPWATER: Eh?

HUNTER: Or by inference?

UPWATER: By inference.

HUNTER: Then you must be a supernaturalist. I hope I have succeeded in explaining why.

RANGER: I once heard it suggested that truth itself may be evolving.

SANDERSON: All the same I hope you won't press it just now. For one thing, it will start Hunter off again. No offence, Hunter! Personally I could go on listening for hours—and not only for the pleasure of it. It's like having a new backbone put in. But perhaps we might move on? Otherwise we shall have him explaining, Ranger, that, just as we cannot measure distance without a fixed standard of measurement—and could never measure it at all if we only had a yardstick that kept on changing—so, if truth itself were something that changed, we could never know whether any idea (including that one about truth evolving) is true or not. Thus bringing us back, rightly I am sure, to absolute truth or nothing.

HUNTER: For this relief much thanks!

SANDERSON: I was wondering if we could approach in another way the question we seem to have got to, which is: whether Upwater and all the rest of us are dualists, or supernaturalists, or not. Hunter says we must be; because, while we are speaking, we all assume—whatever we may say to the contrary—that the ideas we are putting forward are not produced by natural causes and are thus not a part of nature. I wonder if it may not be possible for thinking to be a part of nature without its having been *produced* by her? Couldn't it be somehow correlative to nature? (I would say 'existentially correlative', if I was quite sure I knew what 'existentially' means.)

HUNTER: He spoke of a mindless universe *generating* mind.

BRODIE: But I notice he kept open a sort of escape-hatch about thought having possibly been 'latent' or 'potential' in the universe from the beginning; although he also said he doubted it. He might climb out of the difficulty through that.

UPWATER: Thank you. I don't know that I'm aware of any climbing being needed. But I daresay I shall think further of it.

HUNTER: I have nothing to do with 'latent' or unconscious thought. It's a worse contradiction in terms than 'planned evolution'.

BURROWS: I'm interested here. You say that very confidently, but conscious thought is *always* evolving from unconscious. As much perhaps as seven-eighths of our thinking *is* unconscious. If there is one thing modern psychology can claim to have proved, it's that.

HUNTER: All the same, the expression is meaningless. You might as well talk about 'unconscious consciousness'.

BURROWS: We do—and we call it 'the sub-conscious'.

HUNTER: Possibly—but are you in fact talking about anything at all when you use the term?

DUNN: This is getting interesting.

SANDERSON: What happens to our minds when we are asleep?

HUNTER: They are not there. There is nothing to talk about.

DUNN: Forgive me saying so, but that is the most reliable observation I have heard this evening.

SANDERSON: Do you mean, Hunter, that the part which you say cannot have been produced by Upwater's 'nature', is born or created afresh every morning?

HUNTER: I don't know. No doubt God could work in that way, if He chose. But the answer is: 'I don't know.' Do you?

Sanderson made no reply. I thought I saw a way of leading the discussion towards a territory where I am a little more at home. 'Are what we call "conscious",' I said, 'and what we call "unconscious" really as totally contradictory—as mutually exclusive as they sound—like Box and Cox—so that the one has to go out the instant the other comes in? I should have thought not; although I agree of course with Hunter about the cleavage between an a and a b—between experience itself and what is experienced—which is the essence of consciousness.'

SANDERSON: May I point out a possible source of confusion? Hunter was mainly concerned to answer Upwater; and in doing so he was talking about reason. It was the cleavage he insisted on between

reason and nature which made Upwater call him a
dualist or supernaturalist. (I gather we are using the
two as synonyms.) But then, towards the end, I suspect
he remembered Ranger's earlier remark about the
mind being the same as the brain. You remember
you stopped him from commenting on it at the time.
And this may have led him on into refuting a rather
different heresy. I am thinking of the behaviourists
and some of the language philosophers who deny
that there is such a thing as 'consciousness' at all—
anyway in its ordinary sense of some sort of private
world of experience, to which the public has no
access. I hope I am not overstating it. Perhaps we shall
hear more about it from Dunn. I confess I thought
we had finished with behaviourism some years ago,
but it does seem to have taken a new lease of life from
the development of Cybernetics and I think 'feed-back'
was one of the words Hunter said we could go on
gabbling till we were black in the face. My point is,
that we seem to be identifying consciousness—any
sort of consciousness, however 'mere'—with thinking—
in the sense of reasoning. What about the consciousness
of the lower animals? I doubt whether any of us
would call that reasoning or even thinking.

BURGEON: Thank you. But don't let's start talking about
'instinct'. Not *yet*, anyway. Let's put the consciousness
of animals into the fourth tray.

BRODIE: Fourth tray?

BURGEON: A Civil Servant used to keep four trays on his
desk to put his papers in. The first was marked

Incoming, the second *Outgoing*, the third *Pending* and the fourth: *Too difficult*.

DUNN: Is it so difficult? The difference between animal and human responses can be summed up in one word: *delay*.

BURGEON: Yes. And I would like to concentrate on that. What happens during that delay, during the interval between stimulus and response? The cleavage Hunter mainly stressed was a cleavage between nature, whether organic or inorganic, and thinking—or thinking in its most characteristic form of reason. And then he said this could never be 'unconscious'; for otherwise we should really be talking about 'unconscious consciousness'. This is, so to speak, where I came in. It didn't worry Burrows; but from something else he said I gather Burrows is not much interested in thinking, except as a way out for the feelings. The question I'd like to consider now is this: Accepting— what shall I call it?—accepting Hunter on Validity—can there nevertheless be such a process as unconscious thinking, and, if so, what is its relation to reason or to what he called 'the whole concatenation of human thought'?

It's a question on which a good deal of work has been done by people who are interested, in one way or another, in symbols. Some of them, who have approached it from very different directions, seem to have arrived at pretty much the same conclusions. For instance, you can approach it through criticism of art and poetry.

DUNN: I thought we were talking about thought. If we are going off into art criticism, it's going to be hopelessly discursive.

BURGEON: What an odd word *discursive* is—meaning two precisely opposite things! But that's by the way. You mean it in the bad sense. Well——

BURROWS: I don't see how art and the symbols in art can be excluded from any inquiry that involves human psychology. Any more than you can exclude myth. Where you have a symbol, you have a meaning of some sort.

SANDERSON: Surely the relation between art and knowledge is a point on which we are at least entitled to keep our minds open. Goethe, you may remember, described art as the mediator between unknown laws operating in the object and unknown laws operating in the subject.

BURGEON: Yes. And I suspect a very definite relation between the 'cleavage' we were talking about—and what is sometimes called 'distance' by writers on aesthetics. But I don't want to go into all that and anyway I'm not capable of it. I hardly know how to put what I have in mind—and it's a jumble rather than a coherent system—shortly and clearly enough to be worthy of this circle.

Poetry comes into it, because anyone who is interested in the *genesis* of poetry—the art of poetic composition—finds himself pondering on the mystery of thought at its *emergent* stage—the point at which it first appears, perhaps very dimly and vaguely, in

the poet's consciousness. Many poets themselves—
Coleridge and Walter de la Mare, for example—have
been fascinated by the problem. But don't let us start
there. Since evolution is in the air and behaviourism
has been mentioned, I will try and start from that
end, and in that framework. In fact I won't altogether
shirk the fourth tray after all.

I suppose we should all agree that it is possible to
grade living organisms according to the elaborateness
and complexity of their perceptual systems. You
get the very low organisms which have to rely on
contact for information of any sort about their
environment, and the scale rises through the faculty
of perception at a distance, such as takes place in
seeing and hearing, to the stage at which an organism
becomes able to deal with—manipulate—perceptions
when they are no longer actually present. Call them
'after-images', 'memory', 'representations', 'ideas' or
what you like. It seems obvious to me that this is
the earliest stage at which anything that could be
called 'cognition' enters into the question. I mean
the earliest stage *in the scale.* Whether it also came
first chronologically is a separate question. I suppose,
too, that it can fairly be called the human stage. It is
true that the higher animals take precautions, and thus
seem to manipulate possibilities as distinct from actual
situations. How careful cats are not to leave any
traces of their sanitary arrangements if they can help
it! But we cannot imagine a cat *deliberating* about the
best way of doing this. And that seems to be the line

between thinking and instinct. Deliberation is applied only to ideas.

But some of the people interested in symbols have detected a further process that takes place in the human organism. Something that is neither deliberation nor instinct. A sort of pre-conscious deliberation; a manipulation, or ordering, or reconciling of impulses and ideas before they cross the threshold of consciousness. It may come logically *between* deliberation and instinct, but some of them—L. L. Thurston for instance—place it highest and grade human beings themselves by the degree to which they possess this faculty. A man who can only deal with his impulses and relate them to ideas, at the stage when he has become fully aware of them is, they maintain, a lower type than the man who organizes them—how shall I put it?—pre-cognitively. And it is this latter type which culminates in what we call a 'genius'! Perhaps in a poet. The point I am getting towards is, that the ideas or images which have arisen from these—sub-liminal—processes are just those which have the characteristics of *symbols*. Ritual, myth, Jung's 'archetypes', poetic metaphors, and a good deal else have been ransacked and examined from this point of view, because the thing they all have in common is symbolic significance. And it is characteristic of a symbol that it has more than one meaning, often many meanings, sometimes contrasted and even opposite meanings, which are somehow reconciled within it—just the sort of thing, in fact, that can happen in the *mind*, but not in the material world from which the symbols are taken. Symbols are always of the inner world.

You may ask what all this has to do with reason, or with rational thought. I am coming to that. Grant for the sake of argument that—still keeping to the terminology of behaviourism—between his receptor system and his effector system (which he shares with the animals) man has this 'symbolic system', as Cassirer calls it. What is its function? Its function is to create that aesthetic 'distance' between himself and the world, which is the very thing that constitutes his humanity. It is what frees him from the world. He is no longer a peninsula pushed out by natural forces. He is a separated island existing in a symbolic universe. Physical reality recedes in proportion as his symbolic activity advances. He objectivizes more and more completely. But the symbols were the product of his own inner activity in the first place and they never really lose that character, however completely his very success in objectifying them may make him forget the fact. Forever afterwards, in dealing with things he is, as Cassirer puts it, 'in a sense conversing with himself'.

Now Susanne Langer, who started by writing a textbook on logic and went on to writing about art and poetry, insists that this specifically human activity— the 'symbolic transformation of experience', as she calls it, is one with the faculty of reason. She denies that there is any fundamental distinction between the kind of symbol I have been talking about and the symbols which logicians talk about—discursive symbols if you like, or between the conceiving of those symbols and the manipulation of them when they have been conceived. She claims in fact that her theory of symbolism assimilates *all* mental activity to reason.

Yet it is obvious that a great deal of this symbolic transformation does go on beneath the level of consciousness. The most elaborate and universal system of symbols we know is language. And it is in association with the symbols which we call *names* that we build up, from childhood on, the coherent world of distinct shapes and objects which we call 'nature'. The 'merest' sense-experience we can imagine ourselves having is also a process of formulation. Whatever else it is—and you must ask Brodie about that—the world that actually meets our senses is not a world of 'things', which we are then invited to speculate on or experiment with. Any world which pure sensation—pure sensitivity to stimuli—could experience must be a mere plethora—what William James tried to suggest with his phrase 'a blooming, buzzing confusion'. Yet we never do in fact consciously experience such a world. We have converted the percepts into concepts, and moreover into *systems* of concepts, before we even know we have been hit by them. As far as our *conscious* experience is concerned, the perceptual world comes over its horizon already organized. But who has done the organizing? What are you going to call this pre-conscious organizing of perceptual experience, which gives us the world as we actually and consciously experience it? Coleridge called it 'primary imagination'. My friend Barfield called it 'figuration'. Langer, who has dealt with it much more fully and authoritatively, calls it 'formulation'. Both of them, and Cassirer and many others, agree that it is the same activity as the activity which we call, when we *are* aware of it—*thinking*.

I felt I had been talking quite long enough and that I had better pause for comments.

'Yes,' said Upwater, 'I find all that interesting, but not very new or startling. And it is not so far outside my "compartment" as I fancy you think. I don't know that it differs very much from the sort of thing that has long been taken for granted by many biologists. Especially those who have gone farthest in investigating the physical basis of mind—the brain and nerves. There is no doubt that the word 'orange' helps us to see an orange. Reports collected from people born blind and subsequently operated on suggest that they do experience something not very far from that "blooming, buzzing confusion", even though they are already familiar with the world through their other senses. And moreover that it is painful. They may take as long as a month to learn the names of even a few objects and, until they have learned them, they are unable to recognize the same object on being presented with it a second time.'

SANDERSON: I can well believe that. It is the symbol which fixes the *concept* of the object, so that the mind not only distinguishes it for a moment from the general flux, but identifies it as that *sort* of object.

UPWATER: As a matter of fact some of the brain people go a good deal farther. They insist that the brain practically *creates* the object. They say that the form we give to the world is a 'construct' of our brain. Isn't that much the same as what Burgeon was saying?

SANDERSON: I would have thought not. For in the way they put it I believe there is no room for any element of *expression*—any continuing imaginal link between inner and outer, which is the essence of a symbol. Moreover, in so far as you insist on talking about the brain instead of the mind, I should have thought you came up against the difficulty that arose between Ranger and Hunter. The series of brains, observing and observed, is rather like the procession of oozlem birds. Each bird consumes the one behind it. But how do you deal with the last bird in the procession, or how does it deal with itself? More seriously, if you start from the *brain* and say it 'constructs' the world it is aware of, you seem to me to leave out of account the fact that the brain as an object of observation is itself part of a world which you yourself have constructed. Surely you have got to *start* with the *act* of construction and not with the brain!

RANGER: This is getting a bit beyond me.

BURGEON: Anyway, what I have been putting forward will hardly fit in with the ordinary picture of evolution. The principal snag is the nature and origin of language. The biologists always assume that it was invented mainly as a means of *communication*—and they generally add that the object of communication was food-getting. They regard any other function of language as incidental. But if my people are right, the symbolizing by man of the outer world was a principal object in itself. The symbols known as words are presentational in the first instance and only afterwards become utilitarian and discursive. Their object is to produce precisely that 'distance'— or 'cleavage' as Hunter called it—between a purely inner experience and an outer world, which all behaviourists, and I think most biologists, struggle so hard to deny.

BURROWS: The much maligned Freud pointed out that human *behaviour* itself is not only a food-getting skill, but is also a language. He said every move is at the same time a gesture.

BURGEON: Did he? That's interesting. I could embroider a bit farther, but it might mount me on my hobby-horse. Stop me if it does. Language, and especially in its early stage, is full of words which refer *both* to an object or event in the sense-world *and* to a content which is inner or mental. 'Purport to refer', if you like, so as not to beg the question. I needn't give examples. All, or practically all, the words in our own language that now refer to inner experience can be traced back to a time when they had an external reference as well—*spirit, understand, right, wrong, sadness:* it doesn't matter which you take; you've only got to look them up in an etymological dictionary. Since Darwin the theory has been that such words originally had only the external reference and that the inner one was added by using them metaphorically. 'Animism' and all that. But anyone who has studied language from within knows that all that is pure speculation and that there is not a shred of evidence for it—not one scintilla of evidence, as my barrister friends are fond of saying—beyond the fact that modern, civilized men do sometimes deliberately create metaphors in that way. Well, I mustn't go on. The whole thing, with its implications, comes out strongest in Cassirer, who is sometimes led into writing almost as if it was not man who created speech, but speech that created man.

SANDERSON: Which is incidentally good Christian theology.

RANGER: I never heard that before.

BURGEON: Well, have a look at the beginning of St. John's Gospel. But the point I *really* meant to make is, that if you accept—as it seems to me you must—this view that what we call the natural world is found, on analysis, to be largely a 'construct' of the human mind, it upsets Hunter's thing. I mean the sort of conception he seemed to be founding on, of reason as a process that is grafted on to a fundamentally irrational universe from outside its workings.

UPWATER: Hear! hear!

HUNTER: Nothing I said ruled out some kind of continued working of the Divine Mind in the external universe.

BURGEON: Possibly not. But you didn't seem to believe that while you were saying it. You did seem to found very much on an absolute contrast between reason on the one hand and an irrational 'nature' going on by itself, on the other. And you stressed very hard that the former, if it is to be valid, must be totally independent of the latter.

UPWATER: He certainly did.

BURGEON: Yes. It's all very well for you to talk, but it upsets your thing just as completely.

UPWATER: I suppose 'my thing', as you call it, is the ordinary theory of evolution? What is the difficulty about it?

BURGEON: I seem to be getting excited. When you spoke of a 'mindless universe', you were assuming an articulate world of objects, which would have been recognizable and nameable by us if we had been there, already existing before men, or even animals, appeared on the scene. Before brains appeared on the scene, if you like it better.

UPWATER: Certainly. Why not? We have to construct our apprehension of them, but that doesn't alter the things themselves.

BURGEON: But that way of putting it lets in again the whole 'copy' theory of knowledge, which is the very thing that the symbolists deny and the cerebral anatomists—and as far as I can see, most other thinkers—also *say* they deny, whenever they find it convenient; though at other times they accept it cheerfully enough.

UPWATER: You are trying to suggest a sort of Berkeleyism—that the world is not there except when it is being perceived?

BURGEON: I don't mind what you call it. I thought you said you and your friends had abandoned 'dualism'! Look here! Chuck symbolism and all that and go back to Brodie. We are up against the old watertight compartments again. There is simply no relation whatever between the world as physical science conceives it and the world as biological science conceives it.

UPWATER: On the contrary there is a very close relation indeed, and one that gets closer every day. All our most recent advances are based on treating the two sciences as one. A modern laboratory, where research is going on into the structure of proteins isn't much like the ordinary man's idea of a chemistry lab, I can tell you. It consists largely of racks of electronic equipment.

BRODIE: I don't think that's quite what Burgeon meant. I fancy he wants to go back to me because *he* is interested in the beginning of thinking and I rather suggested I was interested—I was going to say, in the *end* of thinking—which is what it sometimes looks as though we were coming to; and perhaps the extremes tend to meet.

Most of my colleagues would scold me for talking like this. They think we ought to give up trying to 'know' anything in the classical sense of the word and content ourselves with describing patterns and processes—describing them mathematically, that is. But I doubt any of us here are quite satisfied with that—or we would have stayed away. I believe the sort of difficulty Burgeon has in mind is this; and I'll put it as carefully and non-controversially as I can.

If we accept—or choose to work with—the hypotheses and conclusions of modern science *at all*, then we do in practice confidently assume the existence of an objective world which is in some manner and to some extent independent of our minds. Even Upwater, for all his dislike of dualism, can't help referring sometimes to 'external' nature. Now when we speak, or think, of external nature, we may mean one of two very different things. We may mean *either*:

(*a*) what any ordinary person would assume we mean—the stars, clouds, trees, houses, animals and so forth that we see around us.

Or we may mean:

(*b*) an environment which we never actually perceive without the help of precision instruments—and for the most part never perceive at all, but only *infer* from physical experiments or psychological analysis, or both. We do also assume in practice that it is only nature (*b*) which is independent of our sense-organs and our thinking. I don't think Burgeon's point is to argue that one is more 'real' than the other. It is enough that they are different, and that, whether or no you could have nature (*b*), you certainly could not have nature (*a*) without the presence of human minds, or at least some kind of mind.

SANDERSON: I keep getting mixed up between nature (*a*) and nature (*b*). Can't we use more descriptive labels?

BURGEON: *How* about *mind-nature* and *particle-nature?*

HUNTER: Someone might think them question-begging. Better use *familiar nature* and *inferred nature.*

BRODIE: Very well. Whether or no you could have inferred nature, you certainly could not have familiar nature without the presence of human minds, or at least some kind of mind.

And *yet*, he says, we are told that there was once a 'mindless universe' and moreover that mindless universe is always described by geologists and evolutionists and so forth substantially in terms of familiar nature. Of course there were minor differences—large ferns on the surface instead of coal deposits beneath, and that kind of thing. But that is really beside the point. It seems to me there is a real difficulty. What do you say, Upwater?

UPWATER: Ye-es. I remember I *have* sometimes wondered a little along those lines myself. When I have heard some of my colleagues say that it was classical physics—now superseded—that made it seem *as if* there was a physical world outside us, or that in some sense we literally *create* the world we speak about (and I have heard both and more like it), I believe I *have* gone away and wondered for a moment or two ... if we ought not either *always* or *never* to regard nature as ... that the logical conclusion ... but the plain truth is that, when it comes to the point, I just can't believe it!

BRODIE: Well, you are in good company. But I don't know that that removes the difficulty. It was all very well, as long as we were allowed to treat the 'primary qualities', as they called them—extension, solidity, figure and motion—as included in inferred nature; but when these began to go the same way as the secondary qualities; when even *solidity* turned into a secondary quality, it was bothersome. It teased the great T. H. Huxley himself; and it teased A. N. Whitehead when he was writing his *Science and the Modern World*. I can't recall just how he put it; but it was to the effect that by the end of the seventeenth century, science, or he may have said scientific philosophy, was confronted with the conclusion that 'nature is man's configuration' ; and I think he added that the issue had never been resolved.

BURGEON: Well, but what was his own attitude towards it?

BRODIE: Much the same as Upwater's. I can give you his exact words here. He wrote:

'And yet it is quite unbelievable. This conception of the universe is surely formed in terms of high abstractions and the paradox only arises because we have mistaken our abstractions for concrete realities.'

HUNTER: *Securus judicat orbis terrarum.*

RANGER: Meaning?

HUNTER: We rely on the general judgment of mankind.

DUNN: Or to put it another way, the business of philosophy is common sense.

BURGEON: But I'm not only thinking about the general judgment of mankind. I'm thinking about the other scientists. Whitehead simply *evades* the issue.

HUNTER: Yes. It's a *petitio principii* all right. He relies for
his answer to the question on the very assumption
about which the question was raised—the 'concrete
reality' of things.

BURGEON: Well, I just can't understand it.

BURROWS: May it not be simply the normal reaction of the
human mind to almost *any* new and very unacceptable
idea? We call it a 'defence mechanism'.

Burrows is sometimes a trifle pompous and he spoke as
if he really thought we had never heard of a defence
mechanism before.

'Yes,' I said a little testily and sarcastically, 'I'm all in
favour of undermining the other fellow's argument by calling
it a defence mechanism. But this—this isn't an argument
at all! It's a dismissal—a point-blank refusal to think.'

SANDERSON: Surely that is just what justifies Burrows in
calling it a defence mechanism! It was the same with
Dr. Johnson on one memorable occasion.

HUNTER: When he refuted Berkeley's philosophy by
kicking a stone?

SANDERSON: No. I wasn't thinking of that. I doubt
whether there was anything in Berkeley's philosophy
to upset Johnson's *dearest* convictions. I'm thinking of
the time when he was suddenly confronted by
Boswell with the idea that there might perhaps be
such a subject as comparative religion. Has your
friend got a Boswell among his books, Burgeon? I
believe I could find the passage.

'All the same,' I said, while he was looking along the
shelves, 'it really is pretty odd. How *could* the chap who

delivered the Reith lectures a few years ago—*Doubt and Certainty in Science*, I think they were called—talk in one lecture about "a man-world of observers and the relations between them" and tell us to remember that our favourite "real" world was only invented in the seventeenth century—and then fill the very next lecture with descriptions of the world as it was before man existed?

What world did he think he was talking about? The one that was invented in the seventeenth century, or some other?'

'Here it is,' said Sanderson, who had meanwhile found his Boswell and turned up the passage:

> One evening, when a young gentleman teased him with an account of the infidelity of his servant, who, he said, would not believe the Scriptures, because he could not read them in the original tongues, and be sure they were not invented, 'Why, foolish fellow,' said Johnson, 'has he any better authority for almost everything that he believes?'
>
> *Boswell:* 'Then the vulgar, Sir, never can know they are right, but must submit themselves to the learned.'
>
> *Johnson:* 'To be sure, Sir. The vulgar are the children of the State, and must be taught like children.'
>
> *Boswell:* 'Then, Sir, a poor Turk must be a Mahometan, just as a poor Englishman must be a Christian?'
>
> *Johnson:* 'Why, yes, Sir; and what then? This now is such stuff as I used to talk to my mother, when I first began to think myself a clever fellow; and she ought to have whipped me for it.'

BRODIE: It looks as if you're due a whipping, Burgeon. It's an effective answer, if not a logical one.

BURGEON: No, but seriously. *Is* it simply a defence mechanism? We are not dealing with ordinary people. We are dealing with people with exceptionally alert minds——

HUNTER: Johnson's mind was alert enough!

BURGEON: Yes, but these are alert—or should be—to that very danger. After all, complete open-mindedness and a willingness to accept the new and unacceptable are the very qualities in which scientists are trained. You might almost say they pride themselves on it.

SANDERSON: Personally, I believe there *are* other reasons for it and I believe this is one of them. If you compare the way people think nowadays—I don't mean the ideas they have—something more subtle than that— the *flavour* or constituency of their thoughts—with the way they thought in a time even as recent as the nineteenth century, let alone earlier—the thoughts seem to have a, what shall I say? a *brittle* quality about them. Read a lecture by T. H. Huxley himself or a speech by Gladstone—and then read something by a contemporary exponent of science or a contemporary politician. The thoughts are altogether *thinner.* Your Reith lecturer had his thoughts about the correlative status of nature and the mind—or the brain, as he would no doubt say—he was perhaps even basing an elaborate programme of research on them. But he had never *absorbed* these thoughts. Whereas he *had* absorbed the ordinary picture of evolution—including

Upwater's 'mindless universe'—almost with his mother's milk, simply by being a twentieth-century man. It would have been implicit in almost everything he had heard at school—and before that. His newer and later ideas would have to be more than just—slapped on top, as it were; they would have to be absorbed, before he could seriously contemplate the possibility of their driving out the old rooted ones. The Victorians worried all right—if they got as far as thinking about it at all—when a new idea came into their heads that didn't fit in with the old ones. The trouble today is, that we have all got very clever. I am not being sarcastic. We are no longer capable of thinking deeply, because we think too *quickly*.

BURGEON: The nineteenth century! Do you really think— over a short period like that——

SANDERSON: Remember the accelerating pace of change we were talking about in another connection.

'What about the Greeks,' I said, turning to Hunter. 'Would you say they were slow or quick thinkers?'

HUNTER: It's a difficult question. Both, in a way. No one could ever accuse them of being *slow-witted*, whether one thinks of their politics or a dialogue like the *Parmenides*. But I sometimes wonder if they didn't enjoy the *act* of thinking in a way we know nothing of, I suppose because we've got too used to it. I wonder if they didn't almost roll their thoughts round their brains and savour them like vintage port. I am thinking of what happens in a Greek play, when the Chorus stops singing and takes part in the dialogue. It seems to spend most of its time labouring the obvious in a ponderous way—a way that is so ponderous that it must have been intentionally so. There is the whole *genre* of the 'gnomic' utterance which we find it hard to appreciate.

But when I said 'labouring the obvious', I wasn't thinking only of moral saws and platitudes. They often give the same treatment to particular propositions that are both obvious *and* fresh in everyone's mind because someone else has just uttered them. I don't know how this fits in with Sanderson's theory. It comes out even more strongly in Plato's dialogues. It is almost incredible the pains that Plato—or Socrates, as Plato presents him—will take to hammer home the simplest point; how he will keep on at it, long after the greatest numskull in the world must have grasped it thoroughly and be straining at the leash to get on to the next point. Every step in an argument— even when everyone agrees with it at once—has to be illustrated by an analogy, and Socrates rarely contents himself with one analogy. He usually drags in two, or more often three, one after the other, to illustrate the same point. Of course I don't mean the whole of Plato is like that; but there is a very great deal of it.

'Could you give us an example?' said Ranger.

'Not from memory. And I don't imagine this cottage runs to the complete works of Plato.'

'I think I noticed a few Loebs,' I said, 'over there in the corner. See if you can find anything.'

Hunter picked out a volume and began turning over the pages. He stopped and read to himself a little. 'Yes,' he said at last, 'this might do. It's from the dialogue called *Euthyphro*.'

RANGER: What is it about?

HUNTER: It's about Holiness. That's all to the good. There are also dialogues that deal with the sort of thing we have been talking about. But since it's the *method* we want to illustrate, the farther off it is from our subject, the better it will serve. Would you really like me to read a bit? [He looked round.] Very well. They've got to a point where Euthyphro has been asked by Socrates for his definition of holiness. But first of all—yes, that's the best way, I think—[he turned over a page and turned it back again]— Look! This is roughly how the next bit of dialogue would have gone, if it had taken place in this room this evening:

Euthyphro: I define holiness as 'attention to the gods'.

Socrates: What do you mean by 'attention'? You can't for instance mean *looking after* the gods—as we look after domestic animals.

Euthyphro: No. I mean *serving* them—a servant-master relation.

Socrates: But do you really suggest that the gods *need* our services? In what way do you think such services could assist or benefit them? Do you, for instance, mean to imply that these services enable the gods to do or create anything which they could not have done or created without them?

That's as far as I need go. Very well. That's about how *we* would have run through it. This is how Socrates and Euthyphro do it.

He began to read in a pleasant, rather sonorous voice:

> *Socrates:* I do not yet understand what you mean by 'attention'. I don't suppose you mean the same kind of attention to the gods which is paid to other things. We say, for example, that not everyone knows how to attend to horses, but only he who is skilled in horsemanship, do we not?
>
> *Euthyphro:* Certainly.
>
> *Socrates:* Then horsemanship is the art of attending to horses?
>
> *Euthyphro:* Yes.
>
> *Socrates:* And not everyone knows how to attend to dogs, but only the huntsman?
>
> *Euthyphro:* That is so.
>
> *Socrates:* Then the huntsman's art is the art of attending to his dogs?
>
> *Euthyphro:* Yes.
>
> *Socrates:* And the oxherd's art is the art of attending to oxen?
>
> *Euthyphro:* Certainly.
>
> *Socrates:* And holiness and piety is the art of attending to the gods? Is that what you mean, Euthyphro?

Euthyphro: Yes.

Socrates: Now does attention always aim to accomplish the same end? I mean something like this: It aims at some good or benefit to the one to whom it is given, as you see that horses, when attended to by the horseman's art are benefited and made better; or don't you think so?

Euthyphro: Yes, I do.

Socrates: And dogs are benefited by the huntsman's art and oxen by the oxherd's and everything else in the same way? Or do you think that care and attention are ever meant for the injury of what is cared for?

Euthyphro: No, by Zeus, I do not.

Socrates: But for its benefit?

Euthyphro: Of course.

Socrates: Then holiness, since it is the art of attending to the gods, is a benefit to the gods, and makes them better? And you would agree that, when you do a holy or pious act, you are making one of the gods better?

Euthyphro: No, by Zeus, not I.

Socrates: Nor do I, Euthyphro, think that is what you meant. Far from it. But I asked what you meant by 'attention to the gods' just because I did not think you meant anything like that.

Euthyphro: You are right, Socrates; that is not what I mean.

Socrates: Well, what kind of attention to the gods is holiness?

Euthyphro: The kind, Socrates, that servants pay to their masters.

Socrates: I understand. It is, you mean, a kind of service to the gods?

Euthyphro: Exactly.

Socrates: Now can you tell me what result the art that serves the physician serves to produce? Is it not health?

Euthyphro: Yes.

Socrates: Weil then; what is it which the art that serves shipbuilders serves to produce?

Euthyphro: Evidently, Socrates, a ship.

Socrates: And that which serves housebuilders serves to produce a house?

Euthyphro: Yes.

Socrates: Then tell me, my friend; what would the art which serves the gods serve to accomplish? For it is evident that you know, since you say you know more than any other man about matters which have to do with the gods....

'And so on.' Hunter walked across the room and put the book back on the shelf.

'And that,' said Burrows, 'is the way Sanderson thinks we ought to have been talking this evening?'

SANDERSON: Nonsense. I didn't say anything of the sort. Nor do I think so. It was Burgeon who brought the Greeks into it.

RANGER: All the same I know what I'd like—but I expect it's asking too much. I suppose you might say I'm used to dealing with high velocities, and I suppose I am. But at least we know where we are, in space. When it comes to the sort of thing that has been going on this evening, you gentlemen have the advantage of me. Sometimes I seemed to get hold of it—and I confess I found it more interesting than I expected—but then I lost it again. And while I was trying to pick up the thread, you had got on to something else. What I *would* like, is to hear whatever it is Burgeon and Upwater—or Burgeon and Brodie and Upwater—have been talking about taken through again rather in that way and at about that speed.

'That's an *excellent* idea,' said Hunter, slapping his knee. 'I can see I'm going to enjoy this. Come on, Burgeon, it'll be child's play for you.'

'That's all right about child's play,' I said. 'It's not so easy as it sounds. I'm not Socrates. It would want a lot of preparation.'

'Personally,' said Upwater, 'I'd like to hear it attempted. But we'd better not have three of us in it. It would be too difficult to keep it in shape. Burgeon and Brodie get the parts, I think, with the rest of us in the audience.'

Brodie looked at his watch and then across at me. 'It's after midnight,' he said. 'Will you and I volunteer to wash up the coffee-cups and lay to-morrow's breakfast for the four of us staying in the cottage, and talk it over while we're doing it?'

Nobody appearing to dissent from either of these propositions, I got up and switched off the tape-recorder. Whisky and soda was produced for those who wanted it,

and shortly afterwards Ranger, Burrows, Dunn and
Sanderson departed for the town and their hotel in Dunn's
large car with the shabby body and perfectly tuned engine.
After they had gone Hunter again pressed Brodie and me
on no account to lose the opportunity which Ranger had
given us, and Upwater supported him firmly, though
with less enthusiasm. They then retired to bed, leaving us
to do the chores.

As a washer-up Brodie was methodical, thorough and
slow and by the time we had finished the job and laid the
breakfast, we had succeeded in sketching the outline of a
semi-Socratic dialogue which we felt it might be worth
while trying to put up before the others in the morning.
Brodie has his own dry brand of humour behind his large
and solemn face, and he suggested some ways in which
we might add a touch of spice to the proceedings. He
then retired to bed, taking (I was pleased to observe) a
volume of Plato with him. But I was nervous about it
and, after he had gone, I sat up till three o'clock jotting
down some ideas that occurred to me, and trying to get
the whole thing into shape.

SECOND DAY

THE RAIN CEASED during the night and in the morning the sun was shining warmly down from a clear blue sky—a little too clear, perhaps, to give any lasting promise. Soon after breakfast the other four arrived and we all agreed that it would be pleasanter to carry on the proceedings in the garden. Chairs were carried out on to the little lawn and placed in the shade of two trees growing near the house, and garden chairs were found and added to them; luckily there was enough flex on the tape-recorder to get it into a fairly viable position between us.

'Well,' said Hunter, lighting his pipe after we were all seated, 'are you ready? Which of you is to be Socrates?'

'Neither of us,' said Brodie. 'But Burgeon will ask most of the questions. He is used to cross-examination.'

'Yes,' I said, 'he insisted on it—very decently, I thought. But the real reason is, that I have the advantage of genuine ignorance.'

'Ah!' said Hunter. 'I see it's begun already.' And he settled down in his chair.

'Wait a minute,' I said and (wishing very much that this particular task at this particular moment had fallen to someone else) I got up and switched on the tape-recorder. In the dead silence that followed I returned to my chair and began in what sounded to my own ears an odiously self-conscious voice.

BURGEON: Let us begin, my dear Brodie, with the stars. For it is always right to begin with that which is nearest to the gods.

BRODIE: I warned you of this last night, man. You've no need to pretend you actually *are* Socrates. It will only land us in a clanjamfray of anachronisms.

BURGEON: Oh, sorry! Yes, you're quite right. I'll try not to. Well then—did we all agree yesterday that a very great change occurred three or four hundred years ago in the opinions which men hold about the stars?

BRODIE: Yes.

BURGEON: You're too quick! I was going on to say: Or did we agree that this was not the case and that the opinions of man about the stars are the same now as they were five hundred years ago?

UPWATER: I wouldn't overdo it.

DUNN: Or we shall be going on all day and all night.

RANGER: You could start slowing down later on. I really have got that point without difficulty. We did agree just as you say.

BURGEON: All right, all right. But I hope there won't be too many interruptions from the audience. I'm losing my grip. It was our young friend Ranger, was it not, Brodie, who first drew our attention so eloquently to this change of opinion?

BRODIE: Yes, and he was right. We all know the sort of unsupported fancies that underlay the ancient astronomy.

What sort of fancies do you mean?

Well, for instance, that the planets are gods, or the bodies of gods, or are steered through the sky by gods; that all the heavenly bodies revolve round the earth in perfect circles; in nine concentric spheres and so on. *Spheres*, mind you; and the earth itself was well known to be spherical. I mention that, because Ranger said something yesterday about a belief that the earth was flat.

I am surprised that you have not added something else to your impressive list of the opinions of the ancients concerning the sky and the stars.

What have you in mind?

I am thinking of the opinion which seems to have arisen in many different parts of the earth, where men interested themselves in the stars—that the twelve constellations in the ecliptic have each a special quality which is of the greatest importance for mankind.

The Signs of the Zodiac? Yes, I could have added those.

But do not let us occupy ourselves any further with these opinions, since you assure me they were unsupported fancies and you have forgotten more about astronomy than I ever knew. Will you enlighten me, my gifted friend ——

Careful!

Will you tell me, my dear Brodie, what it was that caused men to abandon these opinions? Perhaps they had been formed too hastily in the first place?

I don't see how anyone can know how they were formed in the first place. They had been held for thousands of years.

You astonish me. Many people whom I have met, or whose books I have read, have given a most confident account of how they were formed. Let me see, there was H. G. Wells and even our distinguished friend Upwater, I believe, has no doubts about it. But we must not try to chase more than one hare at a time, in case they should run in different directions. Let us leave alone the question of how these opinions were formed, so that you may have plenty of time to instruct me why they were abandoned three or four hundred years ago.

I think, O Burgeon, that there were a number of reasons all working together.

And may I hear some of them?

It was partly due to the accumulating and increasingly precise records that had been kept for a long time of the movements—I should say the apparent movements—of the moon and the planets through the sky. Tycho Brahe's observations and the records he left of them greatly surpassed in accuracy those of Ptolemy and his predecessors—though these had been good enough for practical purposes such as calendars and the prediction of eclipses. Working with Tycho's material, Kepler was able to prove definitely that the planets move, not in perfect circles, but in ellipses (ellipses round the sun, for Copernicus had already estabhshed that the earth is not the centre of the solar system). That alone was a heavy blow to the old ideas—and Kepler himself didn't much like what he found. But there was another and much more powerful reason. Beginning with Galileo, astronomers became able to *see* the stars—or more particularly the moon and the planets much closer at hand—much more as they actually are.

And how did that come about? Had they grown more sharp-sighted? For I imagine they had none of those devices for travelling towards them, which Ranger was telling us about?

Of course not. But they invented the telescope. And the telescope enables us to see objects which are too far off to be seen at all with the naked eye. Looking through his telescope Galileo saw some of Jupiter's moons. Moreover he could see the details of the moon's surface. All this is an old story. It became obvious that the planets are large solid bodies, like the earth.

And this made it necessary to abandon those old ideas, such as that the planets are the bodies of gods; and ideas about the signs of the Zodiac?

Not this alone. I have left out a very great deal. In addition to what I have mentioned, much hard thinking was done—mainly mathematical in character—and a new understanding grew up of the working of cause and effect.

Dear me! Of what kind was this new understanding? Here am I, over sixty years old, and up till now I had thought that the only thing to be understood about causes and effects is, that the one produces the other. And that, I imagine, was well known before the discovery of the telescope. Or am I wrong about that also?

No. But there are different kinds of causes—or it used
to be believed that there were. Before the time we are
speaking of it was assumed that the stars are not
material bodies at all and that quite different causes
are at work to produce the phenomena in the
heavens from those that are operative on the earth.
And this brings me to the most important change of
all. Besides being an astronomer, Galileo was deeply
interested in the laws of motion. He experimented
extensively in the realm of mechanical and physical
laws. In fact I believe this part of his work is generally
regarded as more important than his astronomical
discoveries and theories. But I do not think we
should go into any more historical details. The long
and the short of it is, that we now know that the
physical causes which we study on earth are the causes
also of the movements of the stars and planets and of
their chemical composition.

Thank you, my friend. And now just tell me this—if I
am not being too importunate.

I shall be happy to tell you all I know, though it is not
very much.

That is extremely good of you. What I am wondering is
this. Do you agree that, when we say we 'know'
anything, we may mean one of two different things?
We may mean that we know it, as I say that I know
how to prove the theorem of Pythagoras about right-
angled triangles; for I was taught it as a boy,
although I have now forgotten it. And I think that,
with a little difficulty and perhaps with the help of

books, I could master it again. Or on the other hand
we may mean that, without any effort of mastery,
our minds are familiar with it as we are familiar with
an old friend and with the thought of him when he is
absent. In this way I know that you have either a belt
or a pair of braces on under that coat you are
wearing, though I cannot see them; or is there some
third way by which men keep their trousers up?

By Zeus, there is no other way that I know of, Burgeon,
besides the two you have just mentioned.

Just tell me this, then. Is the theorem of Pythagoras—
the proof of which requires an effort from us—in
some way less true, or less undoubted, than the fact
that you are wearing a belt or braces?

Certainly not.

Now what I am anxious to know is this. I suppose it is
only very learned men, like yourself, and those
others who study these things themselves with the
help of telescopes and whatever else has been
invented since, who know all those things you have
been telling me about the sky; because of course they
are only known in the first way of knowing?

On the contrary. Even the children's books today tell
much more about the sky we know to be there than
about the one our eyes can see. Every schoolboy
knows, without thinking, that the sky is not a
revolving hollow sphere with points of light stuck
about it in the patterns called constellations. Only the
other day I was trying to point out some of these
constellations (for I happen to be fond of looking at

them) to a schoolboy of my acquaintance, and he
assured me that he was not interested in learning to
recognize them, because they are not real patterns
but only happen to look like that to us. He said
he could not forget that the seven stars in the
constellation called by some the Plough and by others
the Great Bear or King Charles's Wain, are really
enormous bodies of very different sizes scattered
about in space, some of them many billions of miles
farther away from us than others, while among
themselves those that appear to us to be neighbours
are very likely the most distant of all from each other.

It seems, then, that his knowledge of all these abstruse
matters is, after all, knowledge of the second kind.

It certainly looks like it.

Would it be true, do you think, to say that this
youngster's knowledge of astronomy actually makes
it more difficult for him to see these patterns, or
constellations, as we call them? And is this one of
the characteristic effects of knowledge of the second
kind—I mean the sort of effortless knowledge I have
of the fact that you are wearing a belt or braces
which I cannot see?

I think it very likely, Burgeon.

And yet you, who are far more familiar than the
schoolboy with all that you have so generously told
me about the stars, do still see the patterns?

Certainly I do. And so does everyone, I think, who will
take the trouble to look.

Must it not be the case, then (please listen carefully and

correct me if I am wrong), that the sky, or the heavens, or space, or whatever we choose to call it, is not one thing, but two different things?

What two things are you speaking of?

I mean, I suppose, the sky we see and the sky that is really there.

No. I think that what we see is there and that we see what is there.

And so do I think so, my friend. But I see I have expressed myself clumsily and I will try and make my real meaning clearer. Do you see an old cardboard box lying over there in front of the rubbish heap in the corner of the garden?

I do.

It is a rectangular box, is it not?

Yes, it is.

Does that mean that all its angles are right-angles?

It does, O Burgeon.

So that if an artist were making a recognizable picture of it, he would have to take care to make the angles in his picture all right-angles also?

No, of course he wouldn't.

Why not?

Because of the laws of perspective.

You mean he would have to draw on his paper—what shall we say? A lozenge-shaped box?

Yes.

And are these laws of perspective a mere *trompe l'oeil*—tricks based on idle fancies, or are they firmly founded on anything that is really there?

I imagine they are truly based on the fact that that is the way in which the eye sees the box.

Nevertheless we say that the box is really rectangular?

Yes. Because we know that from having seen other boxes in other positions—and with the help of our other senses, such as that of touch.

And also, perhaps (for I am thinking of all we heard yesterday), because we have often thought about boxes, sometimes consciously and sometimes unconsciously—as when we first learnt the meaning of the word 'box'?

Yes. I think I am convinced of that.

What if we are looking at two men, one of whom is one hundred yards away and the other five hundred yards away, but both in the same direction from us, shall we say they are side by side?

It all depends.

Then will you at least agree that, if we do see them side by side, we also see one man very much smaller than the other—hardly bigger than a child in fact?

I suppose so.

And that is how an artist must represent them if he is making a recognizable copy of what both he and we perceive?

Yes, it is.

And did we agree, in the case of the box, that the way in which an artist must draw it, if he is to represent it accurately, is not idle nonsense but is firmly founded on things that are really there?

We did.

And I suppose we meant by that, firstly the box itself and secondly the eye which is looking at it?

Certainly.

Or had we better say the eye and mind which are looking at it?

Let us say that by all means.

Just tell me this. Is it something which the box itself does to us that imparts to it a lozenge-shape?

No. Surely not.

Then apparently it is something which we, with our eyes and minds, do to the box.

That seems to follow.

And the same is true, I imagine, in the case of the two men?

Obviously.

Then do you agree that there are two boxes, both of them real, but that one of them is square and the other lozenge-shaped?

No, I don't.

I am disappointed.

Why?

I was hoping by this devious route to persuade you to agree that there are two skies, one of them a revolving hollow sphere stuck about with brilliant points of light, and the other the sky you were telling me about, which Galileo and others have discovered with their instruments.

Well, I'm afraid you haven't succeeded.

Then how would you like us to put it?

I am not sure, Socrates—Burgeon, I mean.

Let me suggest another way that may suit you better.
We must not say that the hollow sphere stuck about
with points of light is an 'illusion', for you have just
said that when we look at the sky, we see what is
there. And I agreed with you. But there may be
something else we can call it. Shall we say it is also
a 'picture', or a 'semblance', or an 'appearance'?
Which do you prefer? Or is there some other word
altogether that you would like better?

I suppose 'appearance' is the most satisfactory term.
And I believe there is historical warrant for it.

And we should then have to agree, should we not, that
the sky you were describing to me—the one your
schoolboy friend had so firmly in his mind—is—
what shall we say? I suppose it would have to be
some such term as 'the actual facts', or the 'fact of the
matter'. Or shall we call it 'external reality'?

I think most people would agree that any one of the
three would be correct. I am sure that Ranger
would.

Goodness gracious! Excuse me—I am overcome for a
moment.

What is the matter?

What a narrow escape!

What are you talking about?

A truly alarming thought has occurred to me. But, in
order to make you understand it clearly, I fear I shall
have to ask you to imagine for a moment a very
fantastic and impossible state of affairs. May we
return to the box for a little? Just imagine if there

were no way of getting to know about rectangular boxes, except by looking at them from a distance—as we are looking at that cardboard one. Suppose that the other ways you mentioned had not yet been discovered. And then suppose that someone took it on himself to form theories about the nature of boxes, their origin and history and so forth. Would he not be in danger of wasting a great deal of time explaining how some boxes had acquired their distinctive lozenge-shape?

He certainly would—if indeed one can suppose such a thing happening at all.

Yes, my friend, it is very difficult for us to imagine such a thing. For we are in the fortunate position of knowing that boxes are in fact rectangular, and that if one is to theorize about lozenge-shaped boxes, one must first of all remember that they are rectangular and that the lozenge-shape is only an appearance— though it is a real appearance. All the same, if you still have any patience left for my idle fancies, there is another purely hypothetical question I should much like to put to you.

Please go ahead.

If a man—*not* being in the absurd position we supposed just now, but knowing all we have just been saying—were to undertake a study of lozenge-shaped boxes, their nature, origin and history and so forth, ignoring the fact that the lozenge-shape is an appearance, as we have agreed to call it, and omitting any reference to the laws of perspective and to human eyes and minds, would such a man in your opinion be wise or foolish?

In my opinion such a man would be an idiot.

Is that because a history, for example, of lozenge-shaped boxes would have to be at the same time a history of human eyes and minds? Or is it for some other reason?

I agree with the reason you have given.

And what would you think of a natural scientist who, after seeing the two men we spoke of, the one near at hand and the other far off, theorized about the bodies and stature of men in the same way, asking himself how some had come to be tall and some very short?

I should think just the same of course.

And would that also apply to the sky?

How do you mean?

I mean, suppose someone were to devise a history of the sky not as it actually is, but as it appears to our eyes, treating the appearance as though it were the external reality.

I see what you mean. That would be equally inexcusable.

But remember Upwater's warning. Don't overdo it.

When I exclaimed just now, it was because I suddenly remembered all that Upwater had told us about the frontiers of *time* having been burst open by science only just after the same thing had happened to the frontiers of *space*. And I thought what a mercy it was that things happened in that order and not the other way round.

Why do you say that?

As Hunter reminded us, before the frontiers of time were burst, it used to be believed that man and the rest of the world were created together. But we now know (if I understood Ranger and Upwater correctly) that the universe existed very much in its present form for many millions of years before man was generated by it. And indeed histories of the universe are for the greater part histories of those very years. How would it have been, then, if those histories had been written by men who did not yet know that the hollow sphere stuck about with points of light, with a Great and a Little Bear to turn it round and round the Pole Star, is only an appearance and who thought it was the external reality? Would they, do you think, have devised a history of what was happening among hollow spheres and points of light, and the patterns in which these lights are disposed, and about the evolution of Celestial Bears, both great and small, millions of years before there were any human eyes or minds?

I can hardly believe they would have been so stupid.

Nor can I, my friend; but it is fortunate, is it not, that when men began to inquire seriously into the true history of the universe, they knew what it was really like and all about the vast difference there is between the appearance of the sky and the external reality?

Yes, I suppose it is fortunate. But isn't this all rather farfetched?

You put me to shame. A philosopher ought, as you remind me, to avoid indulging in idle fancies. I expect all this wandering about in the sky has made

me a little giddy. Let us return to earth, if you are
agreeable, so that I may learn more about the science
of physics in which you are highly skilled, and of
which I know nothing. Did you not say that it was
this realm—the laws of solid bodies in motion and so
forth—that Galileo examined even more fully and
successfully than he examined the sky?

I did, Burgeon. And I was right.

And no doubt he felt the same sort of relief as I do now
in turning his attention back again from the sky to
the earth. For example, he no longer needed to use a
telescope and I have no doubt he felt an additional
security in being able to rely on his unaided senses.

Well, no. As a matter of fact he was the first man to
make good use of the very similar instrument, the
microscope. Since his time very little progress in
physics has depended on the unaided senses. We
heard something yesterday of the radio-microscope
and other much more complicated developments.

So we did. I have promised to curb my fancy;
otherwise I should have liked to mention yet *another*
foolish idea that has just occurred to me.

You had better let me have it.

I was thinking, my friend, how odd it would have been
if examination of the earth through microscopes had
produced the same sort of result as examination of
the sky through telescopes.

What sort of results do you mean?

Well, you did not agree that we have discovered that
there are two skies. But you did agree that the sky

which our eyes perceive or seem to perceive—the hollow sphere with points of light—is very different from the sky, or space, which you described to me, and you assured me, I think, that the former is an appearance depending on the eyes and minds of men and the latter is the fact of the matter, or, as we agreed to call it, the external reality. Just fancy if, with the help of the microscope and its offspring, we had discovered something of that sort about the earth!

But that is just what we have discovered!

Help! I am growing giddy again.

We now know, beyond any doubt, that all the attributes of the earth which we call qualitative are subjective.

My good friend, you are thinking much too rapidly for me. You will have to tell me, first, when this discovery was made and then, in simpler language, what it amounts to.

I will try to do so, O Burgeon. Here again it was Galileo who led the way. He discovered as the result of his measurements and experiments, that the ideas men had formerly held about the things on earth, the matter of which they are composed and the motions they perform, were mixed up with all sorts of animistic and anthropomorphic fancies. This, he said, was partly because men had hitherto failed to distinguish the primary qualities of matter from the secondary qualities.

But what are these primary and secondary qualities?

The primary qualities are extension in space, figure, solidity, and number. That at least was what Galileo thought. The secondary qualities are everything else we perceive, such as colour, sound, smell, beauty, ugliness and a great many more that could be named. These secondary qualities are dependent for their existence or manifestation on the mind and the senses.

That was a very startling discovery. It must have made a great stir.

It did.

And not among scientists only, I imagine. I am thinking of your schoolboy friend and of books written for children and for the unlettered multitude. I suppose that, just as you told me it happened in the case of the sky, so it did with the earth; so that schoolboys and others are no longer much interested in the earth they perceive, with its colours and sounds and other charming qualities, but only in the external reality.

No. In this case that did not happen—or to nothing like the same extent.

I wonder why not. Especially as in this case it is something we are all very much concerned with, since it is the earth we live and walk about on, whereas the sky is a very long way off and does not much affect us.

Partly, I expect, because there was hardly time for it to happen, before further discoveries of the same sort were made.

Do be careful, my melodramatic instructor. Remember
how easily I am made giddy.

It was discovered that Galileo was wrong, not in
dividing the qualities into primary and secondary,
but in the place where he put the division. We know
now that most of Galileo's primary qualities are in
fact only secondary. Extension, figure and even solidity
have had to be relegated to the same category as
colour and sound and so forth.

Good gracious! If my memory is right, that leaves only
number.

I am afraid so.

Must we say, then, that the only primary quality is
quantity?

If you like to put it that way, yes.

Then perhaps this renewed feeling of giddiness that is
coming over me is excusable. But, tell me, has not this
meant great hardship and disappointment for many
other scientists?

Go on, please.

There are other sciences, are there not, that concern
themselves with the things of earth, in addition to
the science of physics? I am thinking of such
studies as chemistry, botany, zoology, physiology,
geology and the like; but more especially of those
studies by which we reconstruct the remote past
history and the probable origin of the earth. Were
not these for the most part, before the startling
discoveries you have been telling me about, studies
in the history of secondary qualities, which those

who were pursuing the study wrongly assumed to be primary?

Well, yes, they were. That's why, before chemistry got going, you had what they called alchemy. And the same sort of thing in the other sciences.

I wonder if I have *really* understood what you mean by primary and secondary qualities. I have been assuming that in place of 'primary qualities' we could equally well say 'the fact of the matter' or 'external reality' or something like that and *vice versa*, but that in the case of the secondary qualities, though we do not hold them to be unreal, we could not do that because they are also appearances or semblances depending on the senses and the mind or brain of man.

Yes, that is quite right.

Then I repeat that it must have been a great hardship for these learned men that, just about the time when the frontiers of time were burst through and they might have started writing histories of this solid earth and of the solid plants and animals on it and so forth with all their different colours and shapes and other qualities—histories extending back for millions of years instead of only a few thousands— all this great enterprise had to be abandoned.

Why should it be abandoned?

Because henceforth it seems that any history of such things must either be a history of numbers, or quantities, or something of that sort, or else it must be largely a history of men's minds and eyes and their other senses. Whereas if, for example, solidity had not been discovered to be a secondary quality, very learned and exciting accounts could have been given of a solid earth and solid rocks and plants and animals and so forth on its surface, as they were millions of years before men and their minds were generated from them.

You say many such accounts could have been given; but many *have* been given and they are still being given. Masses of evidence have been accumulated and only the details of it are in dispute.

I see. I suppose, then, that this evidence comes to us in some other way than through our senses and our minds?

On the contrary it is because scientific theories are firmly based on the evidence of the senses that we rely on them.

Do you remember, O Brodie, that we were talking about the sky a few minutes ago and I asked you whether men might possibly (mistaking the appearances for the external reality) have devised a history of the appearance as if it were itself an external reality?

I do.

And would such a history have been based on the evidence of their senses or on some other evidence?

It would have been correctly based on their senses. It is their theories that would have been wrong.

Would this have been because these misguided inquirers were relying on their *unaided* senses, whereas the external reality can only be grasped with the aid of telescopes and other precision instruments?

Yes.

Let me see, how many of our senses can we use in the
study of astronomy?

Only the sense of sight.

Oh dear, then instead of saying 'relying on their unaided
senses' I ought really to have said 'relying on one of
their unaided senses'?

You are very precise.

I try to be, Brodie. Perhaps because I am a lawyer; and in
my profession slovenly thinking is a form of negligence
which may land us in an action for damages. Possibly
it would be well if it were the same in yours and all
other professions. But to continue: just before that we
were talking about lozenge-shaped boxes and the like,
you remember. I asked you, I think, what your opinion
would be of a man who, knowing all about perspective
and so forth, *nevertheless* devised a history of boxes
themselves, in order to account for the lozenge-shapes
or some of them which he perceived with one of his
unaided senses. Can you recall your answer?

Yes. I said that such a man would be an idiot.

What about a man who, knowing not through one of
his unaided senses, but with the help of precision
instruments all about the external reality which causes
the appearance we call the sky, should nevertheless
devise a history of that appearance itself—the points
of light and so forth—which left out the mind and
senses of man and began from a time before man
existed? Would he also have to be an idiot?

I think he would, Burgeon.

We agreed, I think, that by 'primary qualities' we mean the same as we mean by 'external reality' and by 'secondary qualities' the same as we mean by 'appearance' or 'appearances'.

Well?

I am just wondering what your opinion is about those men who knowing, not through their unaided senses but with the help of microscopes and other precision instruments, all about the difference between the primary qualities and the secondary qualities of the earth, nevertheless account for those secondary qualities by showing how they came into being before any minds or senses existed.

You have landed me very neatly, if rather laboriously, in your trap. But it just won't do. The whole thing is far too well established. However much they may differ about other things, *that* is taken for granted by everyone. It's the one thing on which absolutely everybody is agreed.

You alarm me very much. For I know only too well what happens to people who examine too closely into things on which absolutely everybody is agreed. For instance, in fifth-century Athens they were given hemlock to drink and we have just heard that in eighteenth-century England they were whipped by their mothers, or told they should have been.

Oh ay! Very much to the point. But have a heart, man! Just think what you are saying! Hardly a week passes without some new book being published containing a fresh theory about some detail or other

of geo-chemical history or biological evolution, or
claiming to throw new light on the whole process.
But no one ever doubts the main outlines, or that,
billions of years before *homo sapiens* appeared, there
was a solid, mineral earth in existence, of the kind we
know. How could they? Resounding speeches about
it all, delivered to the Royal Society or the British
Association and reported in *The Times* are—why
man, they are part of the *landscape!*

Do you think, then, that I shall be given castor oil to
drink or whipped if I go about the place saying the
sort of thing I have just been saying to you?

No. From what I know of the twentieth century I think
something quite different will happen to you.

And what is that?

You will be totally ignored. Indeed the answer to all
you are saying has already been found by learned and
thoughtful men—both scientists and philosophers.

And what is that answer?

It amounts to this: When it comes to the point, all that
guff about primary and secondary qualities turns out
to be a pure abstraction. Evolutionists like our friend
Upwater are serious and resolute men who make it
their business to handle concrete realities.

I am a very slow pupil, my dear Brodie. Have patience
with me, please. Or rather I entreat you to have
compassion on me. For here have we been talking all
this time and I have only just this moment succeeded
in grasping that there are two kinds of reality, only
one of which is concrete.

Yes, I suppose that's a fair way of putting it.

Please teach me how to distinguish between the two kinds. We have already distinguished 'external' realities from others. These concrete realities are, I imagine, in the external class?

Yes.

And how do they differ from other external realities, which are not concrete?

Well....

I see it is not so easy as I expected from the positive way you spoke just now. But perhaps we shall get on better if I make suggestions and you tell me where I am wrong. Is concrete reality, for example, the kind of external reality we know in what I called a little while ago the second way of knowing—the way in which I know that you are wearing a belt or braces; and the other kind—the external reality which is not concrete—the kind we can only know in the first way—the way in which I know the proof of the theorem of Pythagoras?

It might be that.

But I think you emphatically agreed with me then that the theorem of Pythagoras is in no way less true or less undoubted or less real because it requires an effort on our part to master it?

I did. It's not that. It's a question of knowing when to come back to common sense.

O Brodie, do you know, I find the lesson you are trying to teach me now even harder to master than the theorem of Pythagoras? For I really do not even begin to know what you mean. I thought it was Galileo and the inventors and users of precision instruments who had brought us back to common sense out of all those fanciful stories about the gods and so forth, and now I hear that we have to get back to common sense out of Galileo.

What do you mean? I didn't say 'out of Galileo'. You put the words into my mouth.

I was wrong to do so. Let me explain, if I can. It was the pursuit of physical laws which compelled Galileo to distinguish certain primary qualities of matter from other secondary qualities with which physics has no concern?

Well?

But this distinction—and, I suppose, the primary qualities themselves—has since been discovered, or agreed, to be only an abstraction?

Yes.

That is, of no importance for our knowledge of what is and what is not?

Yes, damn you!

And is it now known that the secondary qualities on the other hand are, after all, not only external, like the unimportant primary ones, but also concrete?

Yes.

And are they therefore the most important for our knowledge of what is and what is not?

Oh, I suppose so.

No doubt, then, since that important discovery was made, physics has begun to concern itself more with the secondary qualities again?

It has done nothing of the sort. I ought not to have
agreed that concrete reality is external. It must be
neither external nor internal or something.

Must we say, then, that whatever concrete reality is,
physical science is the only one which does not
concern itself with it?

Certainly not. It would be absurd.

And that concrete reality may be defined as all those
things on the earth or in the sky which can indeed be
investigated perhaps by science, but not by physical
science?

No. Of course not.

Oh dear, then after all I have not even an inkling of
what you yourself and the other learned and
thoughtful men you alluded to just now, mean either
by the 'concrete reality' you are now speaking of or
by the 'abstractions' you were speaking of a moment
ago. Do please come to my assistance.

I am sorry. I cannot put it any more clearly than by
saying that it is a matter of common sense.

Then let us try another way. I have heard it said that
you physicists, though you modestly admit that you
cannot say what electricity is, nevertheless find room
for it without difficulty among the matters you
inquire into. Perhaps this concrete reality is something
of the same kind. I suggest therefore that we leave on
one side the difficult problem of *defining* concrete
reality and assume for the moment that at least there
is such a thing, and furthermore that it is something
other than either the primary qualities or the secondary

qualities we have been speaking of, that is, something
other than either the external reality itself, which you
assure me we discover with the help of precision
instruments, or the appearances, which you agree
depend on our unaided senses and our minds. Let
us assume this for the sake of the inquiry, and then
let us see if we can find room for concrete reality
alongside the other two. For I take it that, when we
were speaking of these just now, you meant all
you said?

I certainly did.

We agreed, I think, that the secondary qualities depend
on our minds and senses. Did you mean by that that
the mind and senses create them out of nothing, or
that they form or construct them in some way out of
materials given to them from without—impressions
or stimuli or something of that sort?

I meant the latter, obviously.

I have just remembered what Upwater told us, namely
that some of the learned men who examine the brain
describe the secondary qualities as a 'construct' of the
brain. Shall we be content with their word, or shall
we find some other?

I think that one will do very well.

Then just let us see what we know about the art of
constructing in general. A beaver constructs dams, I
believe, using as the materials given to it, the trunks
and branches of trees and the like?

I have always understood so, though I have never
seen one.

And when the dam has been constructed, there are two
things, are there not? I mean, on the one hand, the dam
which the beaver has constructed and, on the other
hand, the beaver itself?

Certainly.

If we took the dam to pieces again, should we find
anything other than the materials out of which the
beaver constructed it?

How could we?

You are quite sure? Please think again very carefully,
my friend. Is there not also a third thing?

What third thing do you mean?

I mean, is there not also — somewhere between the beaver
on the one side and his materials on the other — a
second dam — one which very much resembles the
dam we have been speaking of, except that it was not
constructed by the beaver but came into existence of
its own accord?

By Zeus, you are pulling my leg!

I should not presume to do anything of the sort, and I
was never more serious. What about a table which
has been constructed by a carpenter?

In that case also there are two things, the table constructed
by the carpenter and the carpenter himself.

And there is no second table which was not
constructed by the carpenter?

Of course not.

But how is it with those things that are not constructed
by one man, but by many at the same time, and
which only remain in existence while they are being

constructed? I am thinking of such things as the performance of a play or a ballet. Is there a second play or ballet in addition to the one which the performers are performing?

The answer is even more obvious, if that is possible, in this case than in the other two.

And should I in your opinion be talking sense or should I be talking nonsense if I maintained that the performance was already going on before the performers arrived in the theatre or after they had left it?

You would be talking nonsense.

Do you recall that, a little while back, we were talking about the sky and, when I tried to persuade you that there were two skies, you did not agree? It seems from what we have just been saying that you were right. And indeed I thought so at the time, for I was not very serious in my attempt but only trying to find out what you really think. And just now I have been trying to make sure that it *is* what you really think; for all this talk of abstract and concrete has confused me and left me bewildered. We agree, then, that if Galileo and his successors were right and are to be wholly trusted, there is a real sky, investigated by astronomers, which is the fact of the matter, and which is independent of men's minds and senses, and there is also a semblance or appearance beheld by the unaided eyes and minds of men, and these are not two skies but one and the same sky?

I agree.

You also agreed, I think, that there is no other sky,
resembling the appearance but not depending on the
eyes and minds of men, and that it would therefore
be idiotic to devise the history of such a sky?

Yes.

I say, have you changed your mind while we have
been talking or do you still think that the sky and
the earth are governed by the same laws?

Of course I still think so.

I am relieved to hear it; because it was for this reason
that I felt justified in concluding the same thing to
be true of the earth, namely, that there is a real
earth, investigated by physicists, which is the fact of
the matter and the external reality, and which is
independent of men's minds and senses, and there
is also a semblance or appearance depending on or
constructed by the eyes and other senses and the minds
of men, and these are not two earths but one and the
same earth.

That seems to follow.

And do you also agree that—just as there was no
second dam, no second table and no second ballet—
so there can be no externally real second earth,
resembling the appearance, except that it was not
constructed by the minds and senses of men, but
came into existence of its own accord, and that it
would therefore be idiotic to devise the history of
such an earth?

Something has gone wrong somewhere.

Something has indeed gone wrong if, as I myself think,

this 'concrete reality' of which you have spoken and
which is held by learned and thoughtful men to have
existed long before men themselves did, could be no
other than just such an externally real second earth
as we are at present absurdly supposing. For it seems
in very truth that any such second earth could be no
more than a kind of spectre, which the inventive mind
or brain of man has capriciously interposed between
itself, the constructor, and the world of nature which
it confidently tells us is its 'construct'. And if such a
spectre does not and cannot exist even *now*, but is a
mere figment of man's bemused imagination, I pray
you by Zeus and all the other gods, my gifted friend,
to explain to me how it contrived to exist millions of
years ago, before there was such a thing as a brain or
a mind or an imagination to produce for it even the
pretence of existing.

But I think our friends must be weary of listening
to us and I suggest it is time we left off our dialogue
and joined them in sacrificing a cup of coffee and
perhaps a few biscuits to the god of Nature, the
divine Pan, who was appointed, they say, by the
other gods at times to befuddle the wits of men and
lead them astray like cattle, but at other times, and if he
is fitly approached, to strengthen and inspire them to
true philosophy and godlike energy.

There was a pause followed by a gratifying murmur of
applause and a little decorous clapping, during which I
rose and disappeared modestly into the house, followed
by Upwater with offers to help me. He is a generous soul

and his: 'Well, you have certainly made your point!' sounded like music in my ears. 'And forced us to sit on it—for once!' he added reflectively.

We poured and distributed the coffee and, as soon as we were seated again and had started sipping it. Ranger began.

'I say,' he said, 'I really am very grateful to you for going to all that trouble. I don't mean that it was only on my account. But after all I was the one who suggested it. You have made me see that there is a real problem all right; only hardly anyone is aware of it. Certainly not the chaps I work with. But could you clear up one thing I am fogged about? It is this distinction that Brodie made yesterday between familiar nature and inferred nature—although of course there can only be one nature really—at least you both seemed to agree on that.

'I thought, some of the time while you were going into it this morning, that familiar nature was all that we see and so forth with our senses—the qualities; and that inferred nature was the base we arrive at by *thinking* really hard about familiar nature with the help of experiments, that is by science. But some of the time today you were speaking as if familiar nature *also* depended on thinking as well as perceiving. That was where I got fogged.'

BURGEON: We did go into it a bit yesterday, but not so fully as we did into other things. Do you remember it arose out of the question whether there was such a thing as unconscious, or sub-conscious thinking. I began to get rather excited about symbols and imagination, because I said even familiar nature was no more than a blooming, buzzing confusion until we began thinking as well as perceiving. And afterwards Upwater said, Yes, that was all right, but there was nothing very new in it. And he went on to quote some of the things he had heard his colleagues say about the brain creating or constructing the objects it perceives.

RANGER: Yes. But it was new to *me*. I'd never heard anything about it.

BURGEON: Exactly! The watertight compartments again! But I think the true distinction lies between the nature we know of through the unaided senses plus unconscious thinking, which Brodie called (*a*)—and we agreed to call 'familiar nature'—and the nature we know of through the use of artificial aids to the senses and precision instruments plus a very conscious kind of thinking—ratiocination in fact, and of course mathematics—which he called (*b*), and we agreed to call 'inferred nature'.

RANGER: Oh!

HUNTER: I'm afraid I want to ask you a very crude and unphilosophical question. You've had plenty of fun making hay of the twentieth-century canon and rubbing in the inconsistency of the whole scientific approach; and we all enjoyed it very much. At least I did. But do you yourself really believe the world you live in is the kind of world you made it out to be?

BURGEON: And what kind of world is that? Sorry! I've got so used to asking questions instead of answering them. I suppose I know pretty well what you mean.

HUNTER: I mean a world which is a kind of magic-lantern show, projected by our minds and senses on to a backcloth of whirling particles or some mathematical substitute for them.

BURGEON: No. I don't think I do. I never said that I personally accepted it, or I certainly never intended to say so. I was quite genuinely eliciting rather than expounding—eliciting with Brodie's wonderfully self-effacing help. The points we tried to make or rather, as you say, to *rub in*— in the dialogue were (1) that the magic-lantern show both is, and is generally accepted to be, the conclusion which inevitably follows from the premisses underlying the whole development of science since the scientific revolution and (2) that this conclusion is nevertheless overlooked with surprising coolness when it is convenient to do so, and particularly when the past existence of a mindless universe is assumed—as it is by almost everyone. We may reject the conclusion as preposterous, but we can hardly do so without rejecting the premisses. And if we do reject the premisses, we abandon at the same time the whole ground for the major conclusion, that all pre-scientific interpretations of nature were illusory. Personally I have long doubted whether they were anything like as illusory as is generally supposed. But that is not what I am submitting. I am submitting that, whether they were illusory or not, the idea of a mindless universe certainly *is*. There is no difficulty in showing that it will not fit in with the old, traditional interpretations. We have seen that it will not fit in with the new any better. In other words, it's a chimera.

SANDERSON: I liked your word 'spectre' even better.

BURGEON: What it comes to is that the human mind has succeeded in creating a sort of monster, like Frankenstein. Only Frankenstein never got as far as going about telling everybody that the monster existed before he was born and was in fact his father!

SANDERSON: One thing you brought out was quite new to me. I never realized before that it was Galileo himself who introduced the distinction between primary and secondary qualities. Somehow that strikes me as significant.

BRODIE: You mean the maggot was in the apple from the beginning?

SANDERSON: In the apple of the mindless universe—yes.

BURGEON: We seem to be accumulating rather a lot of metaphors.

SANDERSON: All the same, the apple is not a bad one. It was an apple that brought about the Fall in the first instance.

BURROWS: Ah!

HUNTER: That's nothing to do with it. The Fall was a fall into *sin*.

SANDERSON: But surely also into *error*?

BRODIE: Well, maybe they are both as like as one rotten apple is to another.

HUNTER: *Non constat.*

SANDERSON: All the same, Burgeon, now you have stopped 'eliciting', I also would rather like to know what you yourself really believe about inferred nature. You say we can reject the conclusion—the whole structure—if we like, as preposterous. But, as Ranger pointed out yesterday, the point is that it *works*. Do you think it really *is* preposterous?

BURGEON: It works perfectly for purely technological purposes. Not so well, I have suggested, for some others—history and biology and anything to do with living things, or indeed with *qualities* of any sort.

RANGER: I believe I have got your point—that it is nonsense to talk of familiar nature, when there are no minds or senses about to perceive it. But I still can't see what is wrong with describing nature as it *would* have looked to people like ourselves, *if* they had been there.

This time it was my turn to sigh. 'What! After all that rubbing in?' I said. 'Suppose you are right: where is the *point* in doing anything of the sort? We do not try to describe the past history of the Copernican universe by depicting what it *would* have looked like from the earth, *if* there had been an earth and men on it. How would that help? We try to describe what it was *really* like, without reference to the earth. Don't you see how frightfully abstract and remote the method is?'

UPWATER: Why? Let's just see how it works out in practice. We find skeletal remains, from which we infer that there were once flying lizards, or pterodactyls. Their structure moreover indicates a long previous process of evolution. The absence of human remains in the same geological strata indicates that the whole process must have taken place before the coming of man and that these creatures were never beheld by him. Do you say it is all illusion and that there were no such creatures?

SANDERSON: No. No. That is not what he says. Of course creatures existed which deposited these remains. What is unjustified is the assumption, first, that because no physical human remains are found, human consciousness was not yet operative in any form, and, secondly, that terrestrial conditions in general already resembled those of today — *qualitative* conditions, such as the relation between air and water for instance.

UPWATER: I'm afraid I no longer know what you are talking about.

BURGEON: You should. After all, it is your own whole case that nature is *one* huge, delicate process, of which man and his mind are a part; one delicate structure, in which every part is interdependent. What right have you got to abstract one bit and imagine the rest going on just as usual?

UPWATER: If the method is as faulty as you say, why has it been found so convincing by so many people?

BURGEON: It's the sense of proportion that is amiss. The method is convincing in the way a 'shaggy-dog' story is convincing, *If* the dog, or the horse, could have talked, all the rest is natural enough. It might well have talked in just that way. Grant an initial magical device for upsetting the whole structure of nature and the rest follows. The joke lies in ignoring the miracle—and blandly treating the rest as if it were the point!

HUNTER: We still have not heard what you yourself really think about the relation between familiar nature and inferred nature.

BURGEON: I hardly know. I am only inclined, very tentatively, to see an anology between ideas about nature and ideas about language. By analysing a lot of languages the older philologists got down to a sort of bedrock that they called the 'roots of speech'. That was all right; but then they went beyond that and started saying that these roots existed as words, and that they were the first words from which all language originated. I think that has been shown to be quite wrong. The so-called roots of speech did not come first in time; they are the end-products of late analysis. The nineteenth-century philologists—as has been said by someone who knows more about it than I do—'mistook elements for seeds—and called them "roots".'

But the so-called 'roots' continue to be useful enough. You can use them for making very good and very accurate grammars. You can employ those grammars for teaching people to speak and write languages. And you can do all this equally well, in spite of holding quite false theories about what the roots actually *are* and how they came into being. Well, I sometimes wonder if the 'particles', or whatever, are the 'roots' of nature in the same sense only that the grammatical roots are the roots of speech.

RANGER: But look here—suppose we actually *get* to the planets, as it's pretty certain we shall—and perhaps to some of the stars! Surely that will prove that, at least as far as the sky is concerned, inferred nature is the real thing and familiar nature simply an appearance?

HUNTER: I can't see it making a ha'porth of difference. Whatever object you get to, you will either perceive it with your unaided senses (and Burgeon's unconscious thinking, if he must have it) or you will infer things about it from the readings on your precision instruments. Or both.

BURGEON: It will still be familiar nature and/or inferred nature that you will be up against.

BRODIE: It will be almost wholly inferred nature, I fancy. I suppose on the moon there may be a little actual *seeing* through some very stout transparency in the space-ship's windows. We might even get out and walk on it—or our space-suits might walk about on it, with us inside them. But as to the planets—unless our guesses about them are all wrong—I believe the surface temperature of Venus is above the boiling-point of water and Mercury's many times higher, Jupiter would be about minus 140 degrees centigrade, and Saturn colder still.

SANDERSON: It sounds a poor look-out for the unaided senses.

There was silence for a time and it became clear that nobody had anything to add.

'Dunn,' I said, turning on him suddenly, 'what does all this mean to you?'

'I feel,' said Dunn, shifting his position in his chair a little, 'that I have been assisting at a veritable orgy of subjectivism. And I am surprised how much I have enjoyed it. It has really been very good for me. I had quite forgotten that people do still talk about such things—and so earnestly! I had quite forgotten how charming is divine philosophy!

'I had been wondering what is the best point for me to come in at. It is difficult. There is such a very large cloud of confusion about that we could begin almost anywhere. Perhaps it will be best to start by saying something about behaviourism. I do not call myself a behaviourist, but everything that was said about behaviourism yesterday was the product of a common misconception about what those who are called behaviourists really try to do; and this misconception is very relevant to some others which I will deal with later.

'In the first place, then, behaviourism is not "materialism" whatever (if anything) that word means. Cybernetics was also mentioned yesterday, I remember, and I was not surprised. It is true, I think, that the development of that science has intensified popular misconceptions about behaviourism, because the general interest in electronic computers has led to an increase in the practice of comparing machines with brains and brains with machines. People talk about "electronic brains" for short, as you know. The inevitable result has been that all the people who used to enjoy themselves throwing brickbats at "materialism" —

the people with a mystical axe to grind—now aim their brickbats at behaviourism.

'The misconception is a very simple and obvious one. Assuming that it is useful, for a number of purposes, to compare the brain with a machine, it is perfectly legitimate to do so. Considerations of brevity may then also lead to our sometimes actually using about the brain the sort of language we use about machines. And that is also legitimate, provided you never forget that you are now using a kind of shorthand. But that does not mean that we think the brain actually *is* a machine; any more than the fact that we also sometimes compare the brain to a store (and then go on to using about it the language appropriate to the activity of storing) means that we think that the brain actually *is* a kind of warehouse. "Brain" still means brain and nothing else, "machine" means machine, and "warehouse" means warehouse.

'The primary confusion, therefore, the confusion on which the whole issue—or rather the whole supposed issue—between materialism and immaterialism is based, arises from ignorance, or forgetfulness, of the rules governing the use of language. The result of that ignorance or that forgetfulness, which is a very common failing in human beings, is that we keep on using, or purporting to use, a type of language which is appropriate to one set of circumstances, when we are talking about another set. And in that happy way we make the mistake of thinking we are saying something profound when we are really saying nothing at all.'

RANGER: I see we have got back into top gear again. I haven't quite followed all that. Could you give us an example?

Dunn: Certainly. The institution I work in is called a 'university'. If you go to the place you will see a number of buildings scattered about called 'colleges'. Now there is a story of a distinguished coloured visitor to the university who was shown round all the colleges one after another. And, when they gave him to understand that he had seen them all, he asked to be shown the university.

Ranger: I see what you mean. The university is all the colleges taken together. The visitor didn't know that. But surely it is useful to have a single word to use instead of having to go through the list of colleges every time you want to talk about it?

Dunn: That is a very good question. And the answer is: Yes, of course it is. Not only useful but necessary for a large number of practical purposes. The confusion only arises—and this is the moral of the story—if you start fancying that the university is itself one of the colleges, or so much like one of the colleges that you can say things about it which only have any meaning when they are said of college buildings. The word 'university' can be used meaningfully in one class of sentences and the word 'college' in another class of sentences. Transpose the classes; introduce a word like 'university' into a sentence to which only words like 'college' belong, and you will be talking nonsense, though you may believe you are saying something very original and very exciting.

Ranger: You mean a chap must know what he is talking about before he starts in talking about it?

DUNN: I beg your pardon?

RANGER: If we want to say what we mean, we must first know what we mean?

DUNN: I'm afraid it's not quite as simple as that.

RANGER: But surely, if the coloured bloke had understood the meaning of the word 'university', he would never have made the mistake!

DUNN: That is a dangerous way of putting it. Unless of course you know that you are using semantic shorthand; and I very much doubt if you do. Otherwise you are adopting the common error of assuming that the meaning of a word is a sort of invisible something kept inside it, like a kernel in a nut or a monkey in a cage. Something you can take out of the cage and deal with separately from the word itself.

RANGER: But surely you *can*. We have been doing it ourselves.

HUNTER: Is it nonsense to say words 'have' meanings?

DUNN: No, it is tautologous. It is saying no more than that words are words. But it is dangerous, because, put that way, it is apt to lead on to enthusiastic inquiries about when and where the meanings occur. If you see a footprint you are justified in assuming that it was made by a foot, but there is no reason to assume that there is a ghost standing in the footprint now. The fact that we can understand a word or a sentence does not oblige us to infer an imperceptible cause for it.

BURGEON: There is a large set of bulky volumes called the *Oxford Dictionary*, which *seems* to be all about the meanings of words. What, if anything, do you say it is really about?

DUNN: The proper function of a dictionary is to instruct the young or the ignorant in the normal way in which words are used by people in a particular community of speakers. That has to be learnt, just as any other skill has to be learnt.

HUNTER: And for that purpose, I suppose you would say, it quite properly uses semantic shorthand. For convenience it talks *as if* the meaning of words could be considered separately from the words, although they can't. But suppose you had to do it in longhand? How would you tell someone who didn't know the meaning of—well, say of the word *cat*.

DUNN: Putting it in longhand, the meaning of a word is the way it is normally used in a sentence.

HUNTER: Do you mean that the meaning of *cat* is the proper way of filling the gap between 'the' and 'sat' in the incomplete sentence: 'The —— sat on the mat'?

RANGER: At that rate 'cat' would mean the same as 'dog'.

BRODIE: You'd have to take a more limited sentence.

HUNTER: Such as 'Whiskers is the name of my —— who is partial to milk and fish'?

BURGEON: I feel we're getting a bit trivial. I think myself that there is a sense in which you can't distinguish between a word and its meaning. But surely the way you people put it bristles with difficulties, Dunn. For instance there is the stress you lay on the 'normal' use. What do you actually mean by 'normal'?

DUNN: I can't see any difficulty. The normal usage of
words is simply the common usage. As I say, the
way people in fact use them.

BURGEON: Yes. But you began by pointing out that the
way people in fact use them is almost always wrong!

DUNN: Ah! I said it was difficult to know where to
begin. The normal use of words is the way in which
they are commonly used in talking about things
which it is possible to talk about.

HUNTER: The line in which it is most difficult to know
where to begin is a circle. The possibility that that is
the root of your difficulty ought perhaps not to be
altogether ruled out.

DUNN: That's rather offensive, you know.

BURGEON: Oh come! It was agreed that no holds should
be barred. But my mind has been toying with watertight
compartments again and I have been wondering
what the bearing of all this is on the *res gestae*, I mean
on the rest of what we have been talking about. For
we all agree, do we not, that we have been talking
about something? I'm sorry; I really must get out of
that habit. Brodie and I have definitely finished our
frolic. The point is, that I felt from what Dunn just
said that we were on the point of coming on to that.
Do please go on, Dunn.

DUNN: Well, you are right. I *was* just coming to that,
when I was interrupted. And I am afraid I don't
agree that you have been talking about 'something'
most of the time. Of course I didn't say that ordinary
people talking about ordinary things use language

wrongly. There would be no sense in saying such a thing: because the way ordinary people use words *is* language. It is when people try to talk about the kind of things you have been trying to talk about here that they fall into the error of seeking to make language do what it was never intended to do and cannot do. With the result that they utter strings of sentences, which obey all the rules of grammar and syntax, and which they therefore assume to have some meaning, although they are found on analysis to be meaningless.

For instance I have been sitting here listening to words like 'mind' and 'consciousness' being bandied about in all sorts of exciting ways. But unfortunately in almost every case they have been introduced into the kind of sentence where they simply don't belong. 'Mind' is perfectly good shorthand for a familiar series of events. Everybody understands what I mean if I say 'I have a good mind to go for a walk' or even that 'Russell has a better mind than Macmillan'. But shorthand just won't do when you are trying to talk about the *nature* of mind, trying to *know* something about it, hoping to be shown it and have a look at it. If you do that, you at once become like the man who wanted to be shown over the university as well as over the colleges. For there is obviously no such thing. Mind is a name for the way we perform a certain class of actions.

RANGER: But isn't the question whether that is so or not, just one of the things that Hunter and Upwater were talking about?

DUNN: I have no doubt they thought they were. But my
point is, that since that is a thing it is impossible to
talk about, they were not in fact talking about
anything.

RANGER: It *sounded* as if they were.

DUNN: Of course. It always does. That is what leads
people astray.

HUNTER: It does sound a bit, you know, Dunn, as if you
were saying that, if you feel sure a thing is not there,
you can't discuss the question whether it is there
or not.

DUNN: Whether a *thing* is there or not is exactly what
you *can* discuss. But an abstract noun is not a thing.
You have given me some really beautiful examples
for my pupils. For instance, all that talk about the
brain yesterday. No one but a fool would argue that
the *word* 'mind' and the *word* 'brain' mean the same.
But the question whether some supposed thing
called 'the mind' is or is not the same thing as
something else called 'the brain' is a question that
cannot be answered for the simple reason that it
cannot be asked.

RANGER: But it *was* asked!

DUNN: So was the question 'And now where is the
university?' Can't you seen the point? As Hunter
said yesterday, the obvious is the hardest thing of
all to point out to anyone who is genuinely unaware
of it.

SANDERSON: What he actually said was 'to anyone who
has genuinely lost sight of it'. Whether it is obvious

or not, I doubt whether Ranger ever *had* sight of the point you are making. I certainly hadn't.

DUNN: Listen. People play golf. They carry golf-clubs; they make golf-shots; they play it on a golf-course; they may take in a golf magazine. But because there is nothing particularly exciting about golf——

BRODIE: Man! Man! What are you saying?

DUNN: ——because there is nothing mystically exciting about golf—no one ever goes to the length of assuming that there must therefore be a mysterious inner world in which the *real* game of golf goes on, and still less that an invisible entity called 'Golf' (probably spelt with a capital 'G') exists somewhere with the same sort of status as golf-sticks have in the visible world. Now among the activities human beings perform there is the class of mental or, if you like, mind activities. But in this case—I suppose because some people find it warms their hearts—we are told that, in addition to our activities, there is a mysterious place called 'consciousness', not open to the public, where these activities take place, and an invisible entity called 'the mind' itself, existing alongside the body or sitting inside it like a ghost. Analyse what has been said here today and yesterday and you'll find three-quarters of it is traceable to just that confusion. I thought at first that Upwater—and perhaps Ranger—were immune. But even they seem to be weakening under the prevailing influence.

BRODIE: I'm minding what Hunter said yesterday, rather forcefully, about the ultimate gap between consciousness and that *of* which it is conscious. Do you think what he said was untrue?

DUNN: Oh no. It was true because it was tautologous.

RANGER: Tautologous?

DUNN: I really can't educate you, young man, in the vocabulary of linguistic analysis. You had better read something about it. Try Ayer, or Ryle, or John Wisdom. What Hunter said amounted to reminding us of the way in which the word 'consciousness' is properly used, if it is used at all. It wouldn't make sense to use it in any other way. When we say someone is conscious, we are saying he is conscious *of* something.

RANGER: But didn't you suggest that there was something wrong somewhere?

DUNN: What is wrong is the mystical antithesis which most people go on to infer between the public, physical world and a private mental world of our own, which we call 'consciousness'.

HUNTER: As a matter of fact it *was* that antithesis I was trying to rub in. Only I call it obvious and you call it mystical.

BURGEON: Do you say that our feelings and sensations also are part of the public, physical world? We are certainly conscious of them.

DUNN: Certainly I do.

RANGER: Physical if you like, but surely not public! Otherwise you and Burgeon would feel my stomach-ache.

DUNN: Of course it would not be true to say that Burgeon and I feel your stomach-ache. But neither would it be untrue. It would not make sense. Stomach-ache is just not a word that can be used in that way.

RANGER: It defeats me.

HUNTER: Do you seriously maintain that 'stomach-ache' is an abstract noun?

DUNN: As Ranger was seeking to use it, yes.

BRODIE: In other words there is really no such thing!

DUNN: The operative word being 'thing'.

HUNTER: Very well, cut out the word 'thing'. But surely it *is* a matter of immediate experience that there are some sensations which we share with others and some which we don't! If Ranger and I are looking at the Matterhorn together, and he has stomach-ache, we have the Matterhorn in common but not the stomache-ache.

DUNN: You are adopting the ancient error into which most philosophers have fallen, of assuming that perception is made up of sensations. What is the evidence for it? You are assuming that, when you see something, you first of all have a lot of tiny sensations, like little stomach-aches (which you probably call *sense-data)* and that you then put these together somehow. Is that a matter of immediate experience to you? It is not to me.

HUNTER: I should have thought there was a good deal of evidence for it—neurological and otherwise.

DUNN: I thought we were trying to get down to immediate experience. It is not long since you were pointing out to Ranger that any theory about the brain must start with that. When we look at the Matterhorn, our only sensation is our perception of the Matterhorn. It is no more a compound of other sensations than the sensation of stomach-ache is a compound of other sensations. They are two different sensations and I personally find it no more uplifting to reflect that I do not feel Ranger's stomach-ache than I do to reflect that, when I look at Ranger's stomach, I do not perceive my own.

RANGER: Actually I haven't *got* stomach-ache.

BURGEON: I am glad of it. We have been making a little free, I fear.

DUNN: If we base on experience, we must admit that what we call perception is simply one variety of sensation. It follows from that that sensations are not *components* of perception. Any one perception and any one sensation are both species of the same genus. It follows that the one is not a compound of the other.

SANDERSON: Could you repeat that argument? I would like time to think further of it.

DUNN: Certainly. Perception and sensation are related to one another, not as whole and part, but as two species of the same genus. It follows that one cannot be compounded of the other.

BURGEON: But what about familiar nature and inferred nature? What about the distinction between the qualitative and the quantitative universe, that Brodie and I have been taking so much trouble with? All physical theory is based on it, whether classical or modern. Do you say it is all bunk?

DUNN: Anything that anybody says about perception is an abstraction coming after it, not an experience coming before it.

BURGEON: You stick to the 'concrete reality' in fact.

HUNTER: They used to call it 'naïve realism'.

DUNN: I really don't mind what you call it.

HUNTER: It may be all right if you are prepared to face *all* the consequences. But I very much doubt whether you are.

BURGEON: Surely—quite apart from the consequences—there are great difficulties in the way of equating a perception with a primary sensation! When we perceive the Matterhorn—when we perceive any mountain, knowing it to be a mountain—when we perceive a mountain *as* a mountain and not simply as a splodge, an element of *recognition* enters into the perception itself. I should have thought that was alone enough to differentiate it from sensation.

DUNN: A good deal of unnecessary fuss has been made about recognition. Of course the way we act or react in perceiving depends on the previous state of the organism, as all our other actions and reactions do. And of course every organism is modified by the events in which it is from time to time involved—including the event of perceiving. You can say that it acquires visual and auditory expectation-propensities. Or you can say—in shorthand—that we look at mountains 'in a mountain-seeing frame of mind'. But that does not mean that there is an idea of mountain—a sort of ghostly mountain hidden inside us somewhere that rushes to meet the external one. Any more than the fact that a ticket-machine delivers a ticket and the correct change means anything of that sort.

BURROWS: If I have understood correctly, all this talk about stomach-ache and mountains and ticket-machines is designed to support your previous contention that there is no such thing as a private mental world in each one of us over against the public, physical world which we all have in common. I still don't understand in the least how you can seriously expect any sane person to listen to you. Never mind mountains—what about dreams?

DUNN: That is a matter on which I cannot speak with the authority of personal experience because I myself never do dream. I am always either wide awake or sound asleep. But I do not see any difficulty in it. It is obvious that some animals dream also. If you look at a dog when it is dreaming, the fact that what is going on there is conative behaviour often comes out very clearly.

BURROWS: You are over-simplifying.

BURGEON: 'Conative behaviour'. You say—or I suppose you do—that speaking is simply one variety of physical behaviour, and that it is an illusion to talk of the meanings of words apart from the words themselves. Suppose I pause, while I am speaking, in order to deliberate which of two words will best express my meaning: what do you say is happening then?

DUNN: Much the same as when you pause while you are eating, to decide whether you will take salt or mustard.

BURGEON: It doesn't feel at all the same.

DUNN: Perhaps I had better make clear again what I am saying and what I am not saying. I am not saying that nothing really happens when we deliberate a choice of words or when we dream. I am saying that, *when we are discussing how we know anything, or what we can be said to know,* it is a delusion to talk about meanings and dreams, and so forth, as if they were entities of which anything at all can be predicated. Any such statement is unverifiable, and I mean by that, not that it is untrue, but that it cannot be shown to be either true or false. Therefore it is meaningless. The only statements we can prove true or false are statements about the experience of a normal observer in a normal state of mind. It is only this kind of statement that is a statement about the world and therefore only this kind which is, strictly speaking, a statement at all.

BURROWS: In your sense of the word, nearly every one of the statements made by Freud, for instance, about the unconscious is unverifiable and therefore meaningless.

DUNN: Thou sayest it.

HUNTER: Can you give us an example of a *meaningful* statement?

DUNN: Yes. 'Hunter is sitting on the left-hand side of Brodie.'

HUNTER: What about statements about history?

DUNN: They are meaningful in so far as they are *theoretically* verifiable; that is to say, in so far as they are not of the kind that *could* not be proved true or false.

HUNTER: You seem to be impounding in the word 'theoretically' an implied condition: 'if the past were still present'. It's asking a good deal. I suppose, in the same way, you would say that scientific inferences from artificial aids to perception *could* in theory be verified in your way, *if* we had different kinds of senses, and therefore are not pure abstractions. I cannot for the life of me see why the principle of verification should be stretched all that way to suit you and denied to me when it comes to the immediate experiences of reasoning and private consciousness.

DUNN: The real point is, that you have all been trying to ask what knowledge itself is made of. Knowledge is not made of anything. The 'made' of vocabulary applies to things like pies. It is mearungless to speak of perception as 'made' of sensations, or of sensations and thoughts.

SANDERSON: Meaningless because unverifiable?

DUNN: Meaningless because in its nature both unverifiable and unfalsifiable.

HUNTER: Although statements about a past we can never perceive or about galaxies we can never get to—and could never perceive as a whole, if we did—are somehow meaningful?

DUNN: Can't you see the difference?

RANGER: No.

BURGEON: Well, thank you anyway. Upwater, we haven't heard anything from you for a long time. What do you make of all this?

UPWATER: I don't suppose Dunn will mind my saying that I never felt more dissatisfied in my life. It is *two-dimensional* from beginning to end. I accused you and Brodie and Hunter of taking a 'snapshot' view of man and his problems; but compared with Dunn's, it was positively rich in historical and evolutionary overtones.

DUNN: The fact that you can ask three questions about anything: what it *is*, what *causes* it, and what it *was*, is no reason for mixing them all up together. I have nothing against history or science, but they are not the philosopher's business. His only function is to show how these studies can be pursued without falling into error.

BURGEON: That's all very well, on the assumption that the rules you lay down are really timeless. But yours aren't, you know. For instance, take your definition of meaning: the way words are in fact normally used by normal people. Unless you deliberately shut your eyes to history, you can't get away from the fact that many of them were once used quite differently— especially before the scientific revolution. And since by definition no question arises as to whether they are used rightly or wrongly (except in the special case of philosophical inquiry) it must be not only admitted, but actually part of your case, that words have changed their meanings. To a very considerable extent they have changed them precisely as a *result* of philosophical inquiry. My first objection is, that the rules you are seeking to lay down would prevent any similar change in the future.

DUNN: How do you make that out?

HUNTER: Surely it's plain enough. Before the scientific revolution the word 'gravity', for instance, was used by normal people in a normal state of mind only in the kind of sentence where we should use the word 'weight'; sentences implying limitation to the terrestrial sphere and so forth. If you had been alive when Newton started talking about the law of gravity, you would have had to tell him, if you were doing your job properly, that he was not talking meaningfully, because 'gravity' was a word which simply could not be used in that way.

BURGEON: That helps me to make clear my second objection, which is this. If words like 'gravity', and many others I can think of, had *not* been allowed to change their meanings, we should still be living today in an Aristotelian uiuverse. You can't say: No, we should only *think* we were; because, on your own showing, in a philosophical inquiry we cannot go behind the way words are in fact used by normal people not engaged in such inquiry. And if we cannot do it now, why should they have been able to do it then? But if we *were* still living in an Aristotelian universe, none of the assumptions about language and mind and man's relation to the physical world, on which your whole system is based, would ever have come into being at all.

DUNN: My dear sir, I make no assumptions and I have no system.

BURGEON: Well, but you see, my submission is that you do and have. As to the assumptions, you refuse to look behind the way in which words are used in your own little day, which we have agreed may be called, in shorthand, their meanings. But the meanings of nearly all words are bursting with history and stiff with assumptions. For instance, you made frequent use of the word 'physical' and you used it quite properly as it is used by normal people today. Merely by doing that, you took over *en masse* all the assumptions about the physical world which are current today. As to your system, it seems to me as plain as a pikestaff, and it is no less a system because it is assumed and never argued for. It is no accident that what people now like to call 'linguistic analysis' was fathered by 'logical positivism'; because it grows out of ordinary positivism as naturally as ever a chicken grew out of an egg. It is true that positivism itself is not much of a system and amounts to little more than the uncritical acceptance of the hypotheses of nineteenth-century science. But it *is* a system of assumptions; assumptions of all sorts, including in particular that historical assumption of the origin of mind from a mindless universe, of which we have been talking a good deal here. Everything you say about language is in fact based on that assumption, whether you are aware of it or not; for everything you say about the way language can be used, and the way it cannot

be used, assumes as given the proposition that man
is a tool-using animal and language is one of his
tools. I have suggested that language is something
more than that, but I have not the smallest hope that
I or anyone else will ever convince you of it, because
your method makes the assumption bullet-proof.

BRODIE: Bullet-proof?

BURGEON: Yes. He says, or implies, that language is
no more than one of the tools of a tool-using animal;
and if I or anyone else tries to prove the contrary,
he objects that we are not using language as a tool-
using animal uses tools, and therefore cannot be
listened to!

RANGER: It did sound to me a bit like: Heads I win, tails
you lose!

BURGEON: And lastly—lastly, dash it—you turn and bite
the hand that fed you. I thought that was really
piquante. The whole edifice of positivism, which is
implicit in your use of such words as *physical*, is built
up, from Galileo on, on the assumption that perception
can be analysed into primary sensations. And this
you now have the immortal crust to deny! Don't you
see that you *can't* deny it without denying the whole
positivist system? Alternatively, that if you adhere to
the system, you must accept the concept of perception
on which it is founded? Linguistic analysis my left
foot! It's an outbreak of linguicidal mania! Oh dear!
Sorry, Dunn, I seem to have been letting go a bit. But
do you see what I mean?

DUNN: I hear what you feel—put it that way.

HUNTER: You could equally have added the objection I raised to Upwater's doctrine of mind—especially as here it is handed to us on a plate instead of being wrapped up in a theory of evolution. Consciousness is conative behaviour; and thought is interrupted action. Very well. If that is the case, obviously we can never know that it is the case. Nothing that Dunn has been saying is in favour of it, for nothing he has been saying can be in favour of or against anything. If there is no such thing as discourse, we have not been listening to discourse, but watching his antics and hearing his cries.

DUNN: I've heard that one a good many times before, you know. Hunter.

SANDERSON: I should think you'll hear it a good many times again, until—unless you stop your ears.

Dunn made no reply and we seemed to have come to a natural stop. I therefore raised the practical question of how we were to allot the rest of our time, which extended only to lunch on Sunday, the following day; for some of us had long distances to travel. It had already been settled that we should go into town for our midday meal and we now agreed, after some discussion, that we would take the afternoon off and reassemble after tea. The symposium would then continue as long into the evening as we felt like it, but would in any case end in time for all to eat once more in town; after which there was to be no more until Sunday morning, when we agreed to begin at the same hour. Before we broke up, I asked Burrows to lead off at the evening session and he agreed to do so.

We split up during the afternoon, one or two going for walks in the neighbourhood and others reading or resting. After my late night I felt no compunction in retiring to my room for a sleep, and it was about half-past four when we came together again—indoors this time, as the clouds had been gathering in the July heat and the weather looked as if it might turn to rain.

Apart from Ranger, I suppose Burrows was the least academic member of the party. I do not know what sort of education he had received, but he became deeply interested at a fairly early age in psycho-analysis and I think most of his knowledge of mankind and the world and their history, and indeed of anything else, has been acquired more or less incidentally in the study of that art or science and of the books in which it is expounded. He has been for many years a practising Freudian psychiatrist and a successful one.

'I couldn't help feeling,' he began, 'a tendency here to talk as if there were only three sciences in the world— astronomy, physics and biology. Hunter, for instance, appeared last night to take it for granted that, when science turns its attention to the human being, it must treat him as a biological specimen or a physical object. At least I supposed that was what he meant when he said that science did not know where to stop.'

HUNTER: No. We *are*, among other things, physical objects and biological specimens; and there is no objection to treating us as such for limited purposes. Of course, if you start with the assumption that we are nothing else, the purposes will not *be* limited. If you don't start with that assumption, my objection only arises at the point where you begin treating the 'something else' itself as the object of scientific investigation—followed up of course by experiment and manipulation.

BURROWS: Then I don't agree. If there is one thing we can be sure of, I should have thought it is precisely the fact that reliable knowledge and beneficent practice *in any sphere whatsoever* depend on the application of scientific methods.

HUNTER: Go on.

BURROWS: *You* say, science is losing sight of the human being, I say it is just beginning to find him. We heard a lot about frontiers being broken through—a frontier of space and a frontier of time. But we have heard nothing so far about the third frontier—the latest of the three to be crossed, and in my view the most important. I mean the frontier between the conscious and the unconscious mind. You may not agree that it is the most important. But I think you must at least admit that it is this one which is the biggest *adventure* so far undertaken by the human race, if only because in this case there is a hostile frontier guard to be overcome. Well, perhaps you know what I am going to say; but that doesn't make it any less true. It was Sigmund Freud who first breached the frontier between the conscious and the unconscious and taught us something of the cunning wiles and the invisible power of the censor who guards it. Do I go on to explain what I mean by the 'censor'?

RANGER: You'd have to for me. Would it take long?

BURROWS: I'm afraid it would. What about the rest of you?

BRODIE: I fancy we've all got a working idea of what it means.

HUNTER: You pick it up through the pores these days.

RANGER: Well, go ahead and don't mind me. I daresay I shall pick up enough as you go along. It's a knack I'm beginning to acquire.

BURROWS: Very well. I was going on to say that, since then, the whole territory has been explored by the patient work, both in theory and, still more important, in clinical practice, of a generation of Freud's followers in most of the countries of the world. To anyone familiar with even a small corner of that long story it was an odd experience to listen to a long and apparently serious discussion of the question whether there is or is not such a thing as unconscious thinking. It was like—well, really it was rather like the experience of an adult traveller listening to a group of village children discussing whether there is anything on the other side of the hill behind the village.

As to the incidental question that was raised— I mean, whether the mind should or should not be considered as in some way distinct from the brain, I express no opinion. It's a question to which I doubt if we yet have the answer. But, when Dunn goes on to maintain—at least he *seemed to* be doing so—that there is no such thing as a *conscious* mind, let alone an unconscious one—well, as I said, it is simply not possible to take him seriously. The private world of mental and emotional experience, which he *appears to* deny, is no longer a speculative hypothesis—if it ever was one. It is a field of inquiry, which is being as exactly and painstakingly explored as any other field, though of course we have not yet gone so far as the older sciences have in their own particular fields. Depth-psychology is still the youngest of the sciences, and perhaps there is a case for saying that it suffers from the rashness of youth. But to try and tell anyone who practises it, that the phenomena with which he deals are fictitious, makes as much sense as telling an astronomer that the stars are not there, or an engineer that there is no such thing as steel.

The nearest thing to it I ever met was a patient of mine who took up Zen Buddhism. He started telling me I was all on the wrong lines and that the real point was, not to realize the true self, but to realize that there was no such thing. He left off coming to me.

DUNN: Did you ever hear what happened to him? Did he get well?

BURROWS: Well, yes, he did. I believe he is living a useful, practical life.

DUNN: That's interesting. *A* pupil of mine has just been bitten by it.

BURROWS: What does he say?

DUNN: Oh, I can't remember it all. I know it was something about Samsara and Nirvana; and how it takes most people many lives to learn to disentangle

the one from the other. He said—I must say it was
very decent of him!—that by some kind of grace I
had got beyond all this and arrived at the wisdom
beyond all wisdom; because Nirvana is really to be
found *in* Samsara (which is something like normal
experience), and not beyond it. But he also said I
didn't understand the doctrine of 'Mind-only'. I didn't
think it worth pursuing.

BURGEON: How old is Zen Buddhism?

SANDERSON: It began about the same time as Moham-
medanism. But the enthusiasts will tell you that, just
as Pater said all true art aspires to the condition of
music, so all true Buddhism aspires to Zen, I suspect
they are wrong. But of course there is no stopping
them. If you have made up your mind to throw away
the Jewel in the Lotus, you will throw it away; and it
doesn't matter much whether you call what's left
mind or matter.

BURROWS: Perhaps the philosophically-minded get led
astray by limiting themselves too readily to the *simplest*
examples of what they are discussing. It may be
possible, I don't know, to do something on Dunn's
lines with elementary sensations like stomach-ache,
or even primitive and impulsive emotions like hate
or anger; by leaving out, in fact, precisely the *typical*
examples of private experience, such as the artist's and
the dreamer's. Even then you haven't touched
hallucination and all sorts of psychic phenomena,
such as we know are induced by drugs of the mescalin
type. You have left out mania and mysticism, which

are also under careful investigation, and about which there is a whole library of literature.

DUNN: A library of gush.

BURROWS: Cut out the gush by all means. It still leaves the case-histories. It is just absurd, you know. Well-attested phenomena in all these fields have long been the subject of careful scientific inquiry. I myself am concerned only with the unconscious mind and its relation to the conscious. And this itself is a field which we observe, and with which in some degree we experiment. We base predictions on our observations and experiments; and, above all, we apply the knowledge we gain in practice. No unprejudiced person today can possibly deny the therapeutic efficacy of psychoanalysis.

DUNN: It's not a question of prejudice. It's a question of evidence. According to Eysenck and his followers there are very good reasons indeed for denying it.

UPWATER: Eysenck? His idea of curing human beings is to condition them, as if they were Pavlov's dogs. If he had his way, it would end in destroying all variation, and evolution would be finally arrested at its present stage.

HUNTER: Wouldn't the same result follow from your own project of deliberately controlling heredity?

BURGEON: Just as it would from enforcing Dunn's rules for the use of language!

SANDERSON: In fact you have three different ways, varying from the crude to the subtle, of achieving the same object.

BRODIE: What object?

SANDERSON: The arrest of all further evolution; the freezing of the human spirit into immobility at the outset of its path to maturity.

DUNN: How very impressive!

BURROWS: You will never succeed in making all human beings alike—or by treating them as if they *were* alike. I can say, as a practical man, that, if there is one thing that has been established up to the hilt, it is this: that every human psyche is startlingly different from every other. I am not particularly interested in where the line should be drawn between physical and mental; but I know this, that, psychologically speaking, there is as much variety between the individual members of the human species as there is in the outer world between the innumerable species of the animal and vegetable kingdoms.

SANDERSON: There are some rather important implications in that. But I don't want to interrupt.

BURROWS: I thought your question last night, what happens to our minds when we are asleep, was a good one. After all, we spend about a third of our time asleep, and that is a thing people are apt to forget. When we know more about the mysterious threshold between the unconscious and the conscious mind, we shall probably know more about the threshold between our sleeping and our waking lives.

SANDERSON: Perhaps it is the censor who *sends* us to sleep?

BURROWS: I wouldn't say it is impossible. We simply don't know. Anyway, are our compartments as watertight as Burgeon seems to think? I was very much interested in some of the things he said about symbols, especially when he related them with poetry and art. He spoke of the symbolizing faculty as the fundamentally human one. Here again it was Freud's outstanding discovery, and it has long been established beyond any possible doubt, that the unconscious mind does operate extensively through the symbols which it uses or creates. Largely disordered in dreams; largely ordered by the conscious mind in a work of art. This again is something which Dunn's extraordinary approach seems simply to ignore.

Where I differ from Burgeon is in the complicated inference he seemed to draw from what he said, that our whole theory of evolution must be wrong. I should have thought with Upwater that that, too, was finally established. Burgeon seemed to be attacking it this morning on rather different grounds; but that is a matter for the physicists.

BURGEON: Then the compartments *are* watertight after all!

BURROWS: Well—I heard what you both said. But I had better stick to the things I know something about. As far as any inference of that sort from your 'symbolic faculty' goes, I stick to the rule that, where a simpler explanation is open to us, we should avoid the more complicated or far-fetched one. It is a pity Jung did not do the same. Moreover, in this case the simpler explanation has been well tried and tested. Freud, as you no doubt know, found that most, or perhaps all, of the symbols that appear in dreams can be reduced to infantile experience, which is predominantly physical, and that even the most grandiose imagery, whether it occurs in a dream or in a work of art or in one of the great myths, is usually a pictorial account of primitive bodily functions or their frustration or feared frustration. You may say this is only a theory. But it is a theory that is used in practice—in the practice of mental therapy—and, like Ranger's rockets, it *works*. The proof of the pudding is in the eating.

HUNTER: You mean it sometimes works with the mentally or physically sick. So did the theories of Hippocrates and Galen, but we do not infer from that that they were correct.

SANDERSON: I am more concerned with the fact that it does nothing to account for the *formative* function of symbolism in relation to the outside world, which Burgeon also stressed. For you, it is the conscious mind which does all the ordering; but I remember his pointing out that in some ways the ordering or 'formulation' which occurs at the unconscious level is even more important. He associated it with genius; but he also associated it with the element of mental 'construction' that underlies our normal experience of nature. Perhaps Jung's approach is more satisfactory here?

BURGEON: *More* so, perhaps; but still not very satisfactory. As far as I can make out, when all's said and done, Jung's idea of the myths and the archetypes they embody, is based on some kind of 'projection' by the unconscious mind of its imagery on to a detached and pre-existing outer world of nature. If so, it is our old friend 'animism' all over again. My point throughout has been that any theory of that sort is simply a delusion. It is we, today, who do the 'projecting'. For we assume that familiar nature is and was there without the help of either conscious or unconcious mind. But this assumption is ruled out, *both* by ordinary psychological analysis (as distinct from psycho-analysis) *and* by physical science. It is a delusion and, when we project it back in that way into the past, I call it a 'spectre'.

BURROWS: But so much has been based on Freud's account! As a practising psychiatrist at all events, I see no reason whatever for rejecting suppressed infantile fear and guilt and self-assertion as the bases of our complexes and of the characteristic symbols by which they try to slip past the censor. The Oedipus story is the best known, but it is of course only one of them.

Moreover they go a long way to explain the alternative explanations themselves. The censor takes a hand here too. That was why I said yesterday that you cannot really consider the truth of what a man says without first knowing a good deal about him. For us it is not nearly so much *what* a man thinks that matters as *why* he thinks it.

HUNTER: Oh hell! Have we got to go back over all that again?

BURROWS: I'm afraid, for those who have gone a little below the surface, the evidence for what I am saying

is all too clear. Let me give an example. It was
Burgeon himself who said no holds were to be barred,
so he won't mind my choice. When we hear someone
erecting an elaborate edifice of argument all directed
to show that the solid world around us—a rather
hostile world, isn't it?—is somehow not so solid as it
appears——

BURGEON: That wasn't what I said, but never mind—
go on.

BURROWS: ——and that the mythical-magical idea man
formerly had of nature was perhaps somehow nearer
to the truth; when we find all this tinged with something
like hatred for the idea of a mindless universe—a
rather chilly idea, isn't it?—and accompanied by the
hinted building up of a counter-idea of mind or
thinking as a kind of *ocean*, which pervades us all
and at the same time pervades the outer universe, so
that we can feel at home in it; when this occurs in the
course of discussions during which the paradise-myth
has actually been mentioned, and when it culminates,
and is as it were, summed up, in the highly
significant symbol of an *apple*—well, then, I am afraid
we cannot help reflecting how that old mythical-
magical conception recurs over and over again in the
dreams of our patients; the mythical-magical conception
of nature, which finds expression, above all, in
innumerable myths and cults of the Great Mother.
We cannot help recalling what his own studies in the
history of the alphabet will have made Burgeon
familiar with—how ocean is the *female* symbol *par*

excellence; and we cannot regard it as irrelevant to inquire whether the whole phantasmagoria does not spring from a certain suppressed craving for security, with which we in our profession are very familiar indeed—the longing for a return to the warmth and safety, the *oneness* with our environment, which we *have* all once experienced—in the womb. Well, I could have taken other examples; but one is enough. I do not think it is too much to say that all the recognized philosophies could be reduced in the same way, if we only knew enough. And if that is the case, it is surely stupid to ignore the fact.

HUNTER: I see we *have* got to go through it all over again. Very well, then, here goes. If we——

RANGER: Surely there is still the question whether what Burgeon said is *right* or not.

HUNTER: Thank you, Ranger. Do you keep a dog, Burrows?

BURROWS: No.

HUNTER: If you did, you would probably have tried, as I have with mine, to draw his attention to things by pointing to them. It never works because the old fellow, instead of looking at the thing my finger is pointing to, insists on going on looking at my finger. Isn't that exactly what you are doing?

BURROWS: You have left out of account the fact that the dog has no means of knowing *why* you are pointing.

HUNTER: That has nothing to do with it. The point is, that he doesn't know what pointing *means*. He can't help it; but you psycho-analysts can. He never knew

it. You are training yourselves to forget it. You want
to bring in your superior knowledge. Right. Let us
assume everything you can possibly maintain up to
the limit. Burgeon thinks as he does, because he
wants to be an embryo again; my own aggressive
line is due to frustrated sadist instincts; Dunn denies
his own existence because he is a would-be masochist;
Ranger was crushed by his father, or his mother was,
so he is a power-maniac; Upwater was jealous of his
elder brother, so he wants to go on growing up for
ever and ever; Brodie and Sanderson—I don't know
what there is left for them, perhaps they were
dropped on their heads by their nurses. Assume all
that is true and proved up to the hilt. Assume, further,
that we don't know those secrets about ourselves
because we haven't been psycho-analysed; and that,
if we did know them we should all think differently.
Ranger's point still remains. What we now think
could still be the truth; and if we thought differently,
we *might* then be wrong. The way to find out is to
think, not about *us*, but about what we are saying.

UPWATER: I don't want to be awkward. Hunter, but
yesterday you were rubbing into me equally hard
that, if we know a thought is due to natural causes,
we know it is invalid.

HUNTER: I said we are mistaken if we think it is the
same thing as reasoning. You are justified, for practical
purposes, in ignoring the fancies of a sick man who
has kept on crying wolf because he is sick. But you
are not justified in saying there *cannot* be a wolf

under the bed, because he says there is and he is a sick man. If you want to find out for certain, you must look under the bed and see. Especially if, as Burrows says, we are *all* sick men. I didn't mention the fact, but there is a special irony in my dog's behaviour, because he himself happens to be a 'pointer' by breed. He expects me to understand what *he* means by pointing, though he refuses to admit that I mean anything by it! In the same way—and it's Upwater all over again—Burrows presumably expects what *he* says, including what he says about his patients and about Burgeon here, to be taken as an objective description of what he is talking about and not just as a symptom of his own psychological state. If not, what is the point of anybody saying anything?

SANDERSON: We get back to the difficult business about unconscious thinking. Hunter must be right of course and there is a realm of thought or reason to which we all have common access, irrespective of any self-knowledge, or any lack of it. If someone says the three angles of a triangle are equal to two right-angles, the point is that they *are*, whatever the state of mind or past history of the speaker. And ultimately that must be the point of any statement. The question is, how much of our experience we can get into that clear light. For there is also a much larger realm where our judgments *are* in fact often determined by impulses and so forth of which we are unconscious. Moral judgments are an obvious example, as I am sure Hunter would agree. Indeed it was his whole case that thinking sometimes is caused by natural processes and that, as soon as we know that to be the case, we reject that bit of thinking as invalid. It seems to follow that one way out of invalid thinking, and towards truth, is to acquire knowledge of any natural processes which have hitherto been determining it unbeknown to us. Moral judgments are only one example. If we concede (and I am not sure whether he does or not) that there is such a thing as the unconscious mind and that it has a varying relation to the conscious, I don't see why it should be denied that there may be a very extensive sphere of knowledge in which access to the truth does depend on the degree of *self*-knowledge we may have acquired. Knowledge about the unconscious mind itself would be one obvious example. We shall stop mistaking our own shadow for part of the outside world only when we have learnt to recognize it *as* our own shadow. And we can't do that until we have found out what shape we are. As I understand it, the underlying theory is, that we find out by bringing the unconscious into the light of consciousness. Am I right in thinking. Burrows, that it is a kind of rule for psychiatrists that they themselves must have been psycho-analysed before they practise?

BURROWS: You certainly are.

SANDERSON: Well then, for my part, I feel I must admit that it is *logically possible*—and I don't put it a millimetre higher than that—that, on the sort of subjects Burgeon, for instance, was talking about yesterday, they should be the only reliable 'pointers', the only people who think objectively because their thoughts are not determined by natural causes. Whether it is *actually* possible is another matter altogether. One would have to be satisfied that the kind of thing that goes on in psycho-analysis really does lead to self-knowledge in the sense in which I mean it. Frankly I am not.

BURROWS: You can take it from me that one thing we learn both from our own analysis and from subsequent clinical experience is to recognize a *neurosis* when we see one. If you had listened to as many reports of patients' dreams as I have, let alone the other innumerable reports to be found in the textbooks, you would be in no doubt that all that muddle of totem and tabu, fertility rites and ritual participation, and so forth, which anthropologists find among primitive races, yes, and all the beautiful phantasmagoria of mythology that grew out of it, simply stinks of collective neurosis. There really is no need whatever for any more complicated theory to account for its origin.

BURGEON: *Collective* neurosis! You're working that little word 'collective' rather hard, aren't you?

BURROWS: Neurotics communicate very quickly and sympathetically. I don't mean much more than widespread. If you are suggesting that I was assuming something like Jung's 'collective unconscious', you are mistaken. I don't really know what he means by it and I doubt if anybody does. As I said before, the simpler hypothesis should always be taken in the absence of any compelling reason to the contrary, and the notion

of an unconscious mind, which is 'collective' in the
sense in which Jung sometimes used the word, is
much too complicated for me.

BURGEON: We are beginning to know where we are. I
thought neurosis was a distemper that arises primarily
in highly civilized communities; but perhaps I am
wrong. In any case you are saying, aren't you—to
put it very shortly—that the whole pre-scientific
attitude of man to nature is the product of some
kind of pre-historic trauma? If so, it seems to me you
stand or fall with Upwater. Because you tacitly assume
that pre-historic man found himself surrounded by
something which we should recognize as 'nature',
about which he then formed neurotic theories or on
to which he unconsciously projected his neurotic
fantasies. In saying this, as I have tried to suggest,
you are really saying that pre-historic man was at the
same time post-scientific man, which just won't do. I
am sorry to harp on it, but do you or do you not
accept the spectre of a mindless universe as being
any more than a spectre?

BURROWS: I'm afraid all that is not much in my line. I
have tried to formulate in general terms my reaction
to the sort of thing that has been said here.

BURGEON: If you insist on mentally psycho-analysing me
and refuse to go a step farther—well, there are our
watertight compartments in perfection. Hermetically
sealed!

SANDERSON: I went a good long way with you just now,
Burrows. Can you go a little way with Burgeon? He

has put his position in two entirely different ways. One was yesterday, when he spoke about such things as symbolizing and the origin of language. Symbols are tricky things, and specially related to the unconscious. Perhaps there is a case there for a personally psychological interpretation. Perhaps you'd have to be sure that he knew himself better before you listened to him. Let us anyway grant it for the sake of argument. But the way he put it this morning was quite different. There at least there could be no question of a built-in self-deception. The whole argument, right or wrong, was set in the clear light of reason, and deserves the same sort of attention as a statement that the angles of a triangle are equal to two right-angles. I am not of course saying that it was as self-evident as that, or even that you *must* agree with it. But I am saying that you ought to pay him the compliment of deciding, on its merits, whether you agree with it or not, instead of simply retiring into your shell and trying to think of him as a patient and of his argument as a symptom.

BURROWS: Well, but I should have to do the same for Dunn!

SANDERSON: Well, why not?

BURROWS: If I started taking Burgeon seriously, in the way you mean, I can't foresee where it would end.

SANDERSON: I thought the winkling-out of unconscious motives was rather your speciality!

HUNTER: Yes. Try it on that one!

BURGEON: Womb or no womb, I'd like to go back once more to symbolism before we leave the subject.

Burrows claims that Freud has 'reduced' the characteristic symbols that we find in ancient myths and in many modern dreams to their physical origin. In my view he has done nothing of the sort; because any such reduction is inconsistent with the very nature of a symbol. There is nothing whatever in a physical object or process, as such, that could enable it to stand in our minds for another object or process in the specific manner in which symbols represent or suggest each other. The essence of a true symbol is its multivalence, its quality of meaning a number of different things at the same time. You even get a coincidence of *opposite* meanings. There isn't time to go into examples. But at first a whole generation was quite satisfied that the Greek myths, for example, were simply statements about external nature—'highly figurative conversation about the weather', as Farnell puts it. Another generation interprets them as mainly statements about the unconscious mind. Obviously they were both and neither. Go a little way farther back: dip into the *Vedas* and you often no longer know whether you are reading about birth and death, summer and winter, or breathing in and out. Why? Because symbolic language—and all language is symbolic in origin—can signify all these rhythms at the same time.

Why on earth should language ever have come to be like that, unless it started like that? When I said that there is nothing in physical objects and events that would enable them to stand for each other, I was of course using the word 'physical' as it *is* used normally today. One has to try and say one thing at a time. More precisely, there is *either* no quality like that in them or, if there *is* something, that something is noetic. If it is noetic, it was either 'projected' into or on to them by our minds or it is there intrinsically. As to the fallacy of 'projection', I rather hope we may have disposed of it. I don't see how you can get away from the conclusion that two physical objects and events could not effectively symbolize each other, unless they were both symbols of some original or archetype which is *not* physical (again in the sense in which we use the word today). Symbols which are symbols of the same thing are symbols of one another.

SANDERSON: I agree. The whole of what we call psychology would look quite different if we realized that our own bodies are themselves symbols, in your sense, and perhaps the most characteristic and powerful symbols known to us.

BURGEON: Yes. Mircea Éliade is good on that—and incidentally on Freud himself. Psychologically, what is important to the infant in his mother's body is, not that it belongs to his particular mother, but that through it he makes his first sleepy approach to the *image* of the mother—with all its cosmological and other significances. I think it is in his book, *Images et Symboles*, that he says Freud was so fascinated by his mission that he thought himself the first man to wake up—'le Grand Éveillé'—when he was really only the last positivist. I believe he laid his finger on it there. You are always brought back to positivism,

when you look an inch below the surface of things—
the spectre and his two offspring assumptions: that
the universe is mindless and that man and his mind
derive from an animal origin. That's why I feel
Brodie and I were justified in spending nearly a whole
morning on it. Get rid of that and how much will go
with it! Not only the assumptions, but the assumptions
erected on the assumptions—the whole precarious
card-castle of scientific humanism, for instance.

It was because Freud hadn't got rid of it, as Éliade
points out, that he based on something which has
never existed. In *fact* there has never been such a
thing as 'net' sexuality. Everywhere and always it has
been what Éliade calls a 'multivalent function', with
a primarily cosmological significance. Consequently,
to reduce a psychological situation to its sexual
elements is quite irrelevant to its total significance.
Or rather it is relevant, as any other fact is relevant;
but it has nothing in the remotest degree like the
principal relevance which Freud attributed to it—to
the great delight of the debunking boys! Take that old
gag of the sniggering 'twenties about 'Remember thy
Creator in the days of thy youth'! Of *course* you can
'reduce' it. *Of course* there is a sexual allusion. And
what then? Thanks to this absurd bee in our bonnets,
we are like savages in a cathedral, gaping about us
without a clue to what anything there really means.

Or let me try and find a clearer example. Suppose—
suppose a complete ignoramus, with some reasoning
powers, introduced into a centrally-heated house. He

looks through all the rooms one after another, fiddling idly with everything he sees but understanding nothing. At last he finds himself in the bathroom. He turns on a tap and hot water comes out of it. Hooray! Here at last is something he can understand. Obviously the whole heating-system must be named and interpreted in terms of bathtap. What else could it be? The kitchen-boiler is repressed bathtap; the radiators that warm the drawing-room and the great hall and the staircase are sublimated bathtap; and the airing cupboard is so dry, because it is busy trying to pretend it has nothing to do with the bathtap. As to the origin and explanation of it all. Isn't it obvious that it all grew out of a bathtap? Isn't it obvious that anyone who says otherwise, says so because he has been shut up in an airing-cupboard, where he couldn't see even the pipes, let alone the bathtaps, because of all the clothes and fine linen cluttering it up?

HUNTER: Good.

BURGEON: For the same reason my withers are unwrung by anything Burrows can say about the symbolic significance of oceans and the like, though, even if they *had* been wrung, he would have been quite in order in saying it here. Of course the liquid ocean is a symbol of our origin. It is a symbol of the one spirit, the matterless universe, from which we all sprang— for we certainly did not spring from a mindless one. Of course the physical womb from which we also emerge from unconscious into conscious existence is another symbol of it. And of course the paradise-imago is another symbol of it and one which focuses our nostalgia. Éliade by the way also has good things to say about nostalgia, which for some reason has become almost a dirty word among the highbrows. Every nostalgia, *qua* symbol, is the old *nostalgie du paradis*, and is one of the best things we have got in our psychological make-up—provided of course that we know what it is, and how to use it properly.

RANGER: I'm not sure I know what you mean by 'paradise-imago'.

BURGEON: Oh, simply the various forms in which the imagination of man has clothed his haunting sense that somehow things were once different with him—a Golden Age, before the Fall or before the Flood, when he was still in close touch with nature and the gods.

HUNTER: Avalon, the Islands of the Blest, the lost Atlantis, Saturn's reign——

BRODIE: 'The horns of Elfland faintly blowing'——

RANGER: I remember a story called *At the Back of the North Wind*——

UPWATER: Soria Moria Castle——

DUNN: Nirvana——

SANDERSON: The Land of Shamballa——

BURROWS: The Garden of Eden, in fact——

BURGEON: With the Tree of Life in the midst of it, and Adam still on speaking terms with the beasts. Yes.

I have really had my principal say before and I didn't mean to go on so long. But there is just this to add. It seems to me that the paradise-imago—or myth, or story—is in a way *the* symbol *par excellence*.

I imagine that is why it is so universal and why it has so many ramifying significances. It is the symbol of symbols; because it symbolizes, not so much any single, non-physical archetype, but non-physical existence in general—non-physical existence *as such*. You will never understand symbols until you have grasped that pre-historic man in his unconscious goes back, not to the animal kingdom, as the nineteenth century fondly imagined, but to a paradisal state when there was no death, because there was no matter.

SANDERSON: And which for the same reason could never have been fully realized on earth.

HUNTER: All that is very well, if you accept the Manichean notion that the Fall was a fall into matter. I don't myself, and of course no Christian can.

SANDERSON: I fancy it really depends on what you mean by 'matter'. I should have thought no Christian could deny that matter, as we have made it—with death as its corollary—is the result of the Fall.

HUNTER: Not the most important result. It is a dangerous emphasis—and I don't like it.

BURGEON: Yes, I forgot you were with us! I am quite happy to amend my statement by substituting for the word 'matter' the words 'matter as we understand it and as we have made it'—though I should have thought that was implied.

SANDERSON: I rather hope we shan't get drawn into an argument about Manicheism. It seems to me that any other kind of matter—or rather not any other kind, but any special 'paradisal' matter attributed to a period before the Fall—would be pretty much what Burgeon and I mean by 'spirit'.

DUNN: We are now, I gather, going to begin discussing whether there is, or was, or could be, a thing called 'paradisal matter' and, if so, whether it is the same thing as something else called 'spirit'. *Continuez mes enfants!* Have you got a needle with you, Ranger? I seem to hear the beating of angels' wings.

SANDERSON: Do you know, I sometimes think I see how that old gag about angels on the point of a needle, arose? If it *was* ever said, or anything like it, it was probably in order to startle people; a mental shock, to help them in the difficult business of turning their ordinary ideas inside out.

DUNN: Are you seriously suggesting that that means anything at all?

SANDERSON: Yes. By the way, the fact that the phrase has stuck so persistently in people's memories suggests that it *is* a bit startling. *Was* it ever said, Hunter? I believe you say not.

HUNTER: I only said I have never come across it. But don't imagine I have read through the whole of scholastic philosophy. I know very little of it. It may be there somewhere. The nearest I ever found to it was a passage in Aquinas, where he says:

'Quidam enim imaginationem transcendere non valentes, cogitaverunt indivisibilatem angeli ad modum indivisibilitatis puncti: Et ideo crediderunt quod angelus non posset esse nisi in loco punctali.'

He adds: 'Sed manifeste decepti sunt.'

RANGER: Translation, please.

HUNTER: Certain people, because they were unable to transcend imagination, conceived the indivisibility of an angel in terms of the indivisibility of a point. They inferred from this that an angel could only be in a point in space. But they were obviously wrong.

BURGEON: I suppose 'imagination' in that context means any kind of thinking in images—spatial images?

HUNTER: I think so, yes.

DUNN: Whereas we could of course, if we liked, think in non-spatial images: that is to say, in images which are not images!

BURGEON: I don't see that the concept of a non-spatial image is such an impossible one. For instance, an event in time can function as an image—as Burrows suggests that the story of the Fall does, and as I agree.

SANDERSON: I don't know about images. What I am trying to suggest is that, if you are really going to *think* about spirit, instead of just *talking* about it

BURGEON: Which is what Dunn accuses us of——

SANDERSON: ——you really have got to do something like turning your idea of space inside out. I can't put it much clearer. Rather in the way you are obliged to try and think in projective geometry.

BRODIE: Something about the 'plane at infinity'?

SANDERSON: Which is also a *sphere*. But perhaps more important is the way projective geometry can build up or build down from plane to point—as Euclidean geometry builds up from point to plane.

HUNTER: What has spirit to do with space? It is nowhere and everywhere.

SANDERSON: Yes, but, forgive me, that surely is just words. You surely must admit, since you believe in a Creator, that spirit has some sort of *formative* connection with the objects in space.

HUNTER: Some sort; but we have no way of knowing *what* sort.

SANDERSON: Well, that is just the point. *I* think we have. But, as I say, it means practically turning our ordinary ideas inside out. Suppose I say that spirit occupies a position in space, not by being contained in it, but by containing it?

HUNTER: It is just what Aquinas said. Only he was talking about God.

SANDERSON: But also, I think, about angels?

HUNTER: In another place, yes.

RANGER: I say, does all this matter very much?

SANDERSON: I daresay it doesn't matter very much *now* exactly what St. Thomas Aquinas thought about angels five or six hundred years ago ——

BURGEON: But it may matter a great deal *how* he thought!

BURROWS: Exactly. Isn't that very much what I said?

BURGEON: Well, no. You said, what matters is *why* people think as they do.

SANDERSON: I was going on to say to Ranger that I would have thought it might matter a great deal—especially to people in his calling—to know what different ways there may be of thinking rightly about the nature of space. But I also think it may turn out to matter a good deal to almost everyone. We have been talking about the relation between thinking and nature, or about the relation between spirit and matter. I feel it is much the same problem—unless of course you mean by 'spirit' either the kind of 'ghost' that Dunn is fond of throwing at us, or Hunter's insulated 'Reason'.

Of course we mustn't lose sight of the ordinary way in which words are used and 'spirit' in its ordinary usage could almost be defined as 'not-matter'. But then so can 'unconscious' be defined as 'not-conscious', and I agree with Burrows that, in that case, we shut ourselves out from a whole realm of experience, a whole realm of investigation, a whole realm of reality, if we insist on treating them strictly as Box and Cox. I believe the 'contradiction' between spirit and matter is of the same kind as that between conscious and unconscious; and if you want to learn more about the relation between spirit and matter, the first thing you come up against is the relation between spirit and space. Burgeon said something just now about a 'coincidence of opposites' in the meanings of symbols. There are truths which can only be apprehended by the kind of thinking that is done in pictures—and I believe this relation is one of them. A picture of some sort—even a daft-sounding one like turning space inside out—may be the only way to suggest it; the only way to suggest its *general* nature, that is. Conversely, insistence on logical precision may obliterate it.

Brodie will agree with me, and so I think will Hunter, that they came up against this pretty early in the scientific revolution. We know how the idea of an *empty* space, and of action at a distance, worried Newton. Very wisely, as I think, he set himself to explain—or rather to interpret—all spatial phenomena without bringing in metaphysical or spiritual causes. And for doing that we owe him an inestimable debt. But I dare say that the system of mechanical causality which he developed, just because it seemed so perfect, had a good deal to do with our modern conception of spirit—the Box and Cox one, as Burgeon calls it—as something like 'reason'—something which never enters into space at all; or not at any particular point, or in any way which we can define.

Of course, strictly speaking, mechanical causality rules out the idea of one body acting on another at a distance—which is what is assumed to happen in the case of gravitation. Newton himself was very cautious about this and refused to be drawn into any speculations as to the actual *nature* of gravity.

HUNTER: *Hypotheses non fingo?*

SANDERSON: Exactly.

HUNTER: It means, Ranger: 'I do not invent hypotheses.'

BURGEON: Funny he had to say it in Latin.

HUNTER: Nonsense. It was simply the learned language. Everybody——

BURGEON: I know. I know. I don't mean that. I was thinking how thoroughly English the sentiment is ... the whole English genius popped into three words!

RANGER: How come?

BURGEON: It would take too long. They contain the whole difference between our common law and the Roman law, which the rest of Europe adopted. They might have been spoken by an English High Court Judge.

BRODIE: But not, you'll be saying next, by a Scottish one.

BURGEON: No. *They* went back to Roman law—no doubt because they liked it. I expect it's the Scottish philosophers and scientists who got us all into the mess of abstractions we're in now.

BRODIE: Did you ever trouble to look at Thomas Reid's philosophy of 'common sense'?

BURGEON: No, but I've heard something about it, and I wish I had. I withdraw hurriedly across the border, leaving all your sheep safely grazing. Getting back now to the *res*, I seem to remember that this business of action at a distance bothered the positivists a good deal at one time. They didn't like the word 'force'. Wasn't it Comte who said that the notion of an immaterial 'force' was a relic of animism?

SANDERSON: I should think it very likely. As you know very well, all sorts of surreptitious devices— innocently of course—are used for smuggling back mind into a mindless universe. The biologists do it by suddenly introducing a word like 'copy' or 'information' or 'print off'—or even 'rules'—into the goings-on of genes and chromosomes—or, better still, a technical term like 'engram' or *Gestalt* ——

DUNN: You might call it the 'crypto-noetic' vocabulary.

BURGEON: Excellent. By the way, the fact that an action is 'innocent' does not prevent its being *negligent*, if it is done by someone who ought to have known better. I wish the same rule were applied to theorizing.

SANDERSON: You made that clear to Brodie this morning! I thought you also made very clear the difficulty that arises from this inveterate habit of smuggling, instead of going about it openly. But Galileo—as you also pointed out—was *not* a smuggler. Instead of blinding his eyes to the noetic element in the qualitative processes of familiar nature, he frankly insisted on their presence there, and insisted equally strictly on their *absence* from inferred nature. The result was that the problem of 'action at a distance' still remained as a sort of hedgehog in the garden of inferred nature. That was why classical physics evolved that unsatisfactory notion of 'ether', which it tried for a long time to insist was some kind of material substance filling the whole of space. It's never used now, is it Brodie? But it was an interesting development. If the paradise story is the symbol of symbols, I think we might call 'the ether', as the nineteenth century conceived of it, the spectre of spectres. You find you can't really get on with mindless objects, or mindless process, or empty space, so you invent a sort of 'mindless mind' to fill the gaps.

HUNTER: I am not very happy about the way you and Burgeon keep on using *mind* and *spirit*—and *thinking* as convertible terms. Thinking goes on in *our* minds, and is our act.

SANDERSON: Well, yes—and that is the root of the matter. But will you let me go on in my own slovenly way a little longer? I was going to say that we have got rid of the ether; but we haven't got rid of the other assumption that came in with the notion of mechanical causality.

BRODIE: What is that?

SANDERSON: The assumption that the truth about the structure and origin of things is only to be found by investigating their smallest components; the chase after particles, atoms, molecules, genes, and the way they act on each other. I believe some people insisted that the ether itself was composed of them.

BURGEON: The 'corpuscularian' philosophy, as Coleridge called it.

> The atoms of Democritus,
>   And Newton's particles of light,
> Are sands upon the Red Sea shore
>   Where Israel's tents do shine so bright.

SANDERSON: All right. But let us keep poetry out of it for the moment, please. Everyone agrees that *poetry* must deal with nature as qualitative. It is science we are talking about. The concept of 'ether' seems to have been formed on the analogy of the concept of 'gas', which is itself 'spectral' in Burgeon's sense of the word. The older concept of 'air' as one of the four elements was of course quite different and included a spiritual, and indeed a human connotation. Whereas the concept of 'oxygen', and of 'gas' in general, was expressly designed to exclude anything of the sort.

HUNTER: You are suggesting that this was a mistake—
and that, when matter is *very thin*, it is somehow
more 'spiritual'?

SANDERSON: That may be implied.

HUNTER: Ectoplasm, for instance!

SANDERSON: I don't see why ectoplasm should be dragged
in. I know nothing about ectoplasm and I am talking
about something quite different.

BURGEON: Anyway I don't think such a proposition
would be self-evidently absurd—as I gather Hunter
was suggesting. It is only absurd *if* you begin by
assuming the mindless universe. And that is the
very point at issue. It is obvious that Heraclitus, for
instance, conceived of—and I would say, experienced,
the elements quite differently. For one thing, he held
that he could only perceive them because he also had
them in himself. 'With earth, we behold earth; with
fire, fire; with the ether in ourselves we behold the
divine Ether; with love we behold love and with
hatred, mournful hate.' Not only was heat regarded
as one of the elements, like air, earth and water; but
love and hate were apparently on the same footing
with the elements; and we are hopelessly astray if we
try to understand him on the assumption that, when
he was talking about elements, he meant simply the
material elements, as we have sterilized them.

BRODIE: Is it that way of thinking you are trying to get
us back to, Sanderson?

SANDERSON: No. Because, like Hunter, I find that
thinking is my act—and my *free* act. And I don't

believe I could ever have had that experience if it hadn't been for the scientific revolution; if we had never learnt how to think of the universe as a mindless universe. Heraclitus simply wasn't *able* to think of it that way. If you like to put it so, the elements were still thinking *in* him.

BURGEON: Is this Rudolf Steiner by any chance?

UPWATER: I hope not.

BURGEON: Well, he taught for years in a Rudolf Steiner School, and now the trouble about Sanderson is, that you never know when he is talking Steiner and when he is talking Sanderson.

SANDERSON: We have discussed this before, you know, Burgeon. And I thought I had explained. It's not so simple. For some of us who have been studying him for a long time, Steiner is more like a natural phenomenon than an ordinary writer or lecturer. His output was colossal; and as far as I am concerned, it can be divided roughly into three categories. First, anything he said that I myself have both understood and tested or experienced in some way; for instance, his theory of knowledge, and a good deal of what he has said about the etheric world and about the etheric bodies of living organisms. Secondly—perhaps the largest—the things I feel I more or less understand but cannot say I have ever tested or experienced; for example, his account of telluric and planetary evolution. And, thirdly, the things I can't really say I even understand. We needn't bother with the third. As to everything he said that comes in the second category, though I may have come to accept it for good reasons of my own as undoubtedly true, it would never come naturally to me to repeat it without making its provenance clear, or as though I were speaking in my own person. The first is another matter. I thought I had explained that, after twenty years or so, it really is impossible to distinguish. It is as much Sanderson as Steiner—in the sense that it would be absurd to accuse me of thinking as I do, *because* Steiner thought it also. Just as it would be absurd to accuse Upwater of thinking as he does about evolution simply *because* Darwin or somebody else thought it also. It may be 'because' historically speaking, but, as Hunter has emphasized, any rational thinking stands or falls on its own merits. Causes outside the train of thought itself are irrelevant. I claim no *originality* for anything I have said, or may say—if that's what you mean.

BRODIE: Well, let us go on anyway. I wish I knew more about those old four elements. They lasted right on into the seventeenth century, did they not?

BURGEON: To the end of the Middle Ages—yes. Within the human being himself they still functioned in the form of the four 'temperaments'; though I dare say by that time it was more a matter of tradition than experience.

BRODIE: By the way, Burrows, have you ever looked into it? The old way of thinking wasn't all myths and symbols, I fancy. Can you trace the four elements back to a collective neurosis?

BURROWS: I have never tried to. Probably it could be done.

BURGEON: Oh, it could be done all right; provided the doer had never actually *read* anything written before the seventeenth century, and simply relied on hearsay. I have no doubt it *has* been done. One thing puzzled me, Sanderson. You said something about the elements thinking *in* Heraclitus. And yet you seem to accept the mindless universe. How can you have it both ways?

SANDERSON: I didn't say I accepted the mindless universe as a true statement for all time. I would even go some way with Ranger's friend there, though I was rude enough to shut Ranger up on the subject yesterday. If by 'truth' we mean simply a possible relation between the individual mind and the world——

BURGEON: That *is* the positivist notion of truth.

SANDERSON: I say, *if* we mean that by it, then I don't think it *is* nonsense to speak of truth itself as 'evolving'. If I can 'have it both ways', it is because, like Upwater, I am a firm believer in evolution. Only I think it has always been as much an evolution of consciousness as a geological or biological one. Indeed, if you were right this morning in your exhibition dialogue with Brodie, it is nonsense to suppose you could ever have had the one kind of evolution without the other. I don't see any point in girding at modern science as you are always doing. For me, as for Upwater, it is the stage which the earth's evolution has in fact reached at the moment. The point is, where do we go from here?

UPWATER: Where do *you* say we go—my gifted friend?

SANDERSON: Well, my first answer is: certainly not back to Heraclitus. But my second answer is, that I don't think we can set a course by simply drawing a straight line from the end of the seventeenth century to the first half of the twentieth and producing it. That might lead on and on and on—but hardly up and up and up. If Hunter is right, it must inevitably lead— as it has begun to do already—to systematically *treating* the human being as part of a mindless world. If Dunn is right, or if he is in any way representative, it is already becoming impossible, for many, even to *conceive* of any alternative way of thinking. Moreover, if Burgeon is right, quite apart from any question of human dignity, we shall not even find out *very* much more about nature herself on that straight line, for the simple reason that we have overlooked a basic fallacy in our whole picture of her.

BURGEON: Then it is a fallacy?

SANDERSON: The world-picture of modern science is a fallacy, if we project it back into the past; *and* if we try to fix it for the future.

BRODIE: It is the third answer we would like to hear.

SANDERSON: Well, then—but when you are trying to talk in abstractions about anything as concrete as the operation of mind or thinking in the universe, you get into difficulties, because our whole concept of *time* is itself one of the abstractions. In a way the old relation cannot be said to be there any longer; the Heraclitus one and the still older relation that Burgeon was speaking of yesterday. In a way it can.

Take this very 'ether' we have been talking about. I have just been criticizing the nineteenth-century idea of it, as on the one hand a sort of non-molecular, atomic gas, and, on the other, a sort of 'mindless mind'. Well, so it was.

You can call it a pure invention if you like. But it was quite a useful idea and for quite a time, as Ranger would say, it 'worked'. But there is another 'ether', which is both older and newer. The divine *Aither*, which Heraclitus said he could only experience because it was in himself as well, and which is not an invention. But our approach to it and, because of that, its whole operation in the world of nature, is quite different from Heraclitus's.

And the point is, that it is different *because* of the process of evolution which culminated in what we call the scientific revolution. An evolution of nature, yes, but also an evolution of consciousness, Heraclitus felt the 'ether' in himself, because it was still engaged in making him, as it was still making all men, into an individual thinker with a brain-focused mind. But it has largely finished that process now. We *are* individual thinkers. Our minds *are* brain-focused. Consequently our relation to it is quite different. We cannot sit still and experience it in ourselves. If we want to experience it, we have to go out into it.

RANGER: Isn't that just what we are trying to do today?

SANDERSON: Well, no. I can't agree with that. I think we may find out—*have* found out already—a lot of very interesting and important things by getting out physically into space, if that's what you mean; perhaps even more so by sending precision instruments out. But that is not the *sort* of getting out into space I had in mind. I meant a change in our whole relation, as thinking beings, to space. Without that, however far we may hurl our bodies or our instruments—I think it was Hunter who made this point—we shall still be up against the same old puzzle of familiar nature and inferred nature.

For me the next step which evolution is calling for is something quite different. Once the new, brain-focused centre is created, its whole relation to the periphery changes. In a way it again *becomes* the periphery—or is capable of doing so. By contrast with Heraclitus, *we* can only participate in the 'ether' in what you might call an 'adult' way. This means, not merely looking outward into it and feeling the way it works in nature, including ourselves, but also looking inward *with* it and *understanding* the way it works in nature. That's what I meant when I spoke of turning our idea of space inside out.

HUNTER: I may have got some sort of vague idea of what you are trying to say. I'm not sure. But you seem to me to be constantly confusing two different things— space itself and what you call 'ether' *in* space.

SANDERSON: You can't really separate them. Our idea of space as a vast empty container, like the inside of a packing case, is really quite artificial. I think it will pass. I think it was simply the first impression which a newly-awakened, brain-focused thinking had of its own situation in the universe. For the first time it realized itself as a *centre* in the fullest possible sense of the word. That is why the study of perspective only began at about the same time as the scientific revolution; whereas the practice of visual representation in painting and drawing (which seems to us to call for it so obviously) had been going on for centuries before.

BRODIE: You are really saying there is no such thing as space itself.

HUNTER: There's no difficulty there. Of course there isn't. We only use the word 'space' when we want to think about the *absence* of 'things'. The concept of space is our attempt to think about nothing as though it were something. Wake up, Dunn! You ought to be interested here.

RANGER: You seem to be getting rid of space in much the same way as you got rid of my stomach-ache yesterday.

HUNTER: It was only Dunn who got rid of your stomach-ache—or insisted that it was a public stomach-ache, I forget which.

RANGER: How do you get away from the fact that, when a satellite is sent into orbit, it finds all the space it needs ready waiting for it? And that we can calculate exactly how much it will pass through?

SANDERSON: No, no. You are letting it run away with you. Of course the concept of empty space is necessary for mechanics. Error only creeps in when, because for certain purposes it is right to ignore the etheric aspect of space, we go on to assume that that aspect is non-existent; and that the *nature* of space has never altered and never can alter. That produces what Burgeon would call 'spectral' space.

BURGEON: The very place for rockets!

SANDERSON: The way in which it is convenient to think about space when you are devising a rocket or a satellite may not be the best or truest way of thinking about it when your concern is with quite other things. Let's get back to earth. I believe our idea of space is going to matter a great deal to the way we study living organisms. It is almost literally a matter of life and death there, whether science will continue to think of space *only* in the abstract terms demanded by the particular science of mechanics or also in its etheric aspect.

UPWATER: I just don't see any connection.

SANDERSON: Well, for one thing, if ever there was a science that has been bedevilled by the pursuit of the very small unit, I suppose it's biology. But I'm afraid I did make rather a sudden jump. Really the train of thought, as it has been going on in my mind while I have been listening, is something like this. We began yesterday by talking about space, especially in its astronomical aspect; but we got on fairly quickly from that to the question of the relation between the human mind and the processes of nature. Upwater insisted that that relation could only be understood historically and he told us that mind gradually evolved from an originally mindless universe. But he also suggested that, now it has come, we ought not to think of it simply as the mind of the creature called man, but really as the mind of nature herself; since man is a part of nature. She has made use of the human species, he said, in order to become conscious of herself—or at any rate with that result.

Then, this morning, I thought Burgeon and Brodie made it clear that this picture of an originally mindless universe is an unjustified extrapolation into the past of a familiar nature supposed to be mindless in the present—though the extrapolators themselves also say that there *is* no such mindless familiar nature, and that it was invented in the seventeenth century. They criticized the fundamental inconsistency in all this. And when they had finished their dialogue, there was a strong suggestion that, quite apart from history or evolution, the current view of the relation between the brain and external nature is an impossible one. Someone referred to a 'magic lantern'.

I think everyone agrees that the *idea* of a mindless universe was the product of the scientific revolution. You also agreed that it was found to involve this other idea, namely, that the quantitative universe has to be sharply distinguished from the qualitative, and that it is only the former that is 'mindless'. At least everyone except Dunn seemed to agree about that.

Now I am trying to suggest that this idea of a mindless universe was not a *discovery*, as is generally assumed, of the true state of affairs as it had always been; that is why it is illusory to extrapolate it backwards. But neither was it simply an *error*; that is why it works, when it is applied technologically. I am suggesting, in fact, that this particular idea of the relation between the human mind and the processes of nature, reflects an actual historical change in that relation; or rather a particular *stage* in a change which has been going on since the beginning of time. It wasn't a new idea of the relation between man and nature; it was an idea of the new relation between them.

If I am right, it is not true to say that the human mind, and particularly its less conscious processes, are cut off from the processes of nature because the former go on inside our skins and the latter outside them. But it *is* true to say that the thinking of which we are fully conscious is now focused or centred in the brain in a way which does cut us off from nature and enables us to *feel* ourselves, at any rate, as definitely *not* a part of nature.

HUNTER: Well, it's an interesting speculation, but I don't see how it could ever be more.

SANDERSON: That is where I don't agree with you. I am quite certain that the actual relation between human thinking and the processes of nature can be investigated scientifically.

HUNTER: That won't do. Science proceeds precisely by treating nature as an object, an object from which it *is* cut off.

SANDERSON: Yes. But I thought we had seen that it sometimes gets into difficulties for that very reason. One of the difficulties is, that it finds its hands have been chopped off when it tries to approach anything in nature that is *qualitative*. Suppose it is possible, after all, to investigate qualities in the same conscientious and vigilant way which we have learnt since the scientific revolution to apply to quantities?

BRODIE: How do you apply mathematics to qualities?

SANDERSON: In the sense you probably mean, I don't know that you can. But for me the use of mathematics and of the inductive method are not the essential thing in science. It is the scientific *spirit* that is essential: the regarding of knowledge as an end in itself; absolute open-mindedness; elimination of all personal bias—and the refusal to admit that there is anything which we cannot, or ought not to, know.

BRODIE: I agree, but I don't see where we are getting to.

HUNTER: Nor do I. Moreover, I don't see what all this has got to do with space or 'ether' or anything like it.

UPWATER: Perhaps he can make it a bit clearer.

SANDERSON: I will try, if you really want me to. But I am afraid it will mean your having a good deal of patience with me—or rather a good deal *more* patience. For you've shown quite a lot already.

I sympathize with Dunn [Sanderson closed his eyes for a few moments and leaned back in his chair]; for I also don't quite know where to begin. First of all—as a sort of aside—don't mix up anything I am going to say with the hypothetical 'ether' that came in with the discovery of electricity and the wave-theory of light. I only mentioned that as an interesting historical phenomenon; and I dare say I have confused the issue by doing so.

Then ... well ... let me take it as agreed that all that is *qualitative* in nature does depend for its manifestation on our perceiving and thinking. As Burgeon put it in his dialogue, familiar nature depends on something we *do* to inferred nature—though we do it for the most part unconsciously. However it may have been in the past, it does so depend today. The question whether we can investigate qualities scientifically comes down therefore to the question whether we can investigate this 'doing' scientifically. Now the thinking and perceiving on which the qualities depend are no doubt inextricably mixed. But it is important to distinguish them, because perceiving is a passive and thinking is an active process. As Hunter said, thinking is my *act*. The first question is therefore, whether it is possible to isolate pure thinking and investigate it scientifically.

For Hunter the typical example of pure thinking, isolated from all natural process, and free of any perceptual element, is reason. For me it happens to be mathematics and I prefer to try and consider that. I mean, of course, *pure* mathematics. A good deal of the mathematics in science is not pure in that sense. For instance, in mechanics you'd have to distinguish between analytical mechanics and experimental mechanics. As soon as you start dealing with physical *forces* as distinct from motions, the experimental element enters in. But it would take too long to go into that. You can take as a simple example of what I mean by pure mathematics the theorem of Pythagoras, or almost any proposition of Euclid. The point is that it is something we grasp by a purely inner activity.

HUNTER: I don't know how Dunn deals with what goes on in geometry. I suppose it is impounded in some way under the heading of 'tautology'.

DUNN: I hope at least you don't expect me to be impressed by talk about 'pure thinking free of any perceptual element'.

SANDERSON: Isn't that what mathematics is?

DUNN: I see no reason whatever for saying so. It is a skill that we have to learn, like any other skill—by perceiving and handling things.

HUNTER: How do we learn to think the number 'two'?

DUNN: By perceiving and handling two things, of course.

SANDERSON: How do we learn to think of a triangle—or no, let us say even of a straight line?

DUNN: By perceiving and handling things with straight edges.

SANDERSON: But there *are* no absolutely straight edges in the world outside us. Try looking at even a razor-blade through a microscope!

HUNTER: It's no use, Sanderson. We had better drop it. We can't go over all that ground again. Dunn himself agrees that you can't explain the obvious. Either a man grasps what a concept is, or he doesn't. Well now, you were saying that we apprehend mathematical truth by a purely inner activity. Some of us at least agree with that. Others may do so, when they think further of it. Anyway you had better go on from there.

SANDERSON: Very well. I was going to say that, when we speak of investigating anything scientifically, it signifies that, instead of resting content with a phenomenon as presented to us, we go on to inquire into its *provenance*. We ask how it came about; what was there before that caused it or changed into it. For instance, we rub two bodies together and there is a manifestation of heat. But we do not just say: hulloa, here is heat arrived from nowhere into somewhere! We find out that the heat was latent in the two bodies in another form before it reached the stage of manifestation as heat, and the way in which it was latent, and whatever else that latency involves.

Can we apply the same *principle* to the mathematicizing activity of the human mind?

BURGEON: 'Mathematicizing'?

HUNTER: Try Plato's word 'geometrizing'. It's not so ugly and we can probably take it as applying to pure mathematics of any kind.

SANDERSON: Thank you. I have been a teacher, so I know something about the minds of children. Not much, but a little. It is just a fact that the geometrizing faculty is something that appears in human beings for the first time at a certain definite stage of their development. It appears in fact at about the same time as they change their teeth. The first requirement is, therefore, that we pay attention to this point of time with the same seriousness with which we locate, for example, the melting-point of metals or the boiling-point of water.

The next is, that we go on to trace the provenance of the newly appeared faculty. And if we first train ourselves to do so and then take the trouble to observe it empirically, with the same conscientiousness as we should employ in observing a physical phenomenon, we can observe that it was previously latent in the unconscious depths of the organism. Moreover, if we go on to observe *how* it was latent, and what this latency involved, we can see that, before its appearance in consciousness as a mental faculty, and indeed before the child's birth, it worked *within* the organism, constructively, formatively.

UPWATER: You speak of 'observing'; but how ——

BRODIE: No. Don't interrupt. Let him finish.

SANDERSON: A sort of objective geometrizing, which is engaged in giving to the human form its whole shape and quality—and to the brain the configuration which will be required to support it when it later blossoms as conscious activity.

DUNN: All very remarkable.

SANDERSON: But not more so than the metamorphosis of a caterpillar into a butterfly.

UPWATER: There's something in that.

SANDERSON: And of course it is that conscious activity, that *way* of thinking, when it comes, that will enable

him to confront the external world *as* an external
world—a world which (as we have seen) the mind
has at least to *some* extent, to 'construct' for itself.

I know it all sounds merely theoretical. But that's
because I can't convey the actual *feel* of it. If you are
ever interested enough to want that, you should look
into Harwood's *Recovery of Man in Childhood.*

Meanwhile, if you will assume for the moment
that I am right, the bearing of this on what has been
said before is something like this. The characteristic
form or shape of anything is qualitative. Now the
faculty of observation which we have to develop for
perceiving these qualitative processes—for observing
the operation of the non-physical in the physical—
also reveals that the *form* of anything living, whether
it is a human organism or any other, is not built up
from the centre outwards. You have only to look at
the successive stages of an embryo. It is really an
impossible fancy. Microscopic analysis can never deal
with the form itself; it can at most tell us things
about part of the machinery for transmitting the
form from one generation to another. The form is
built from without inwards. If you really *look* at the
coming into being of form, you are simply forced to
see it that way—as even T. H. Huxley was, when he
looked at a newt's egg hatching.

And that is where the relation between mind and
space comes in. If you really investigate the genesis
of the geometrizing faculty in human beings and
trace it back to its earlier, latent phase, you can no

longer look at a living organism, the way you look at a cardboard box, as an object dumped in an abstract space-time continuum. You are forced to conceive of space as a field, full of latent qualities, an invisibly organized field, a structure-bestowing field, *out* of which the growing organism receives its characteristic shape. You are forced to do so, however difficult our ingrained habits of thought and perception make it at first. I mentioned projective geometry; and that is one useful way of breaking through the perspective habit. (By the way, it's interesting that it grew out of the study of perspective.) But it's not essential. The point is that it is not a physical field of physical forces, but one which is homogeneous with our own thinking.

Perhaps I have put things in the wrong order and should have tried to say this before we go on to mathematics. But the whole emphasis here has been on the relation between *our* thinking and natural processes. So I found myself starting with that. It boils down to this—that there is another way of going about it all besides just *speculating* on the question whether there is such a thing as unconscious thinking, or 'potential mind', or about the relation between our thinking and the qualities of nature. It is also possible to observe potential mind scientifically.

UPWATER: By the way, what *did* Huxley say about the newt's egg?

SANDERSON: I was reading it in bed last night. Wait a minute, I'll fetch it.

He went out of the room and for a while we looked at each other inexpressively in silence. 'I wonder,' said Hunter, 'just where it is we are being led.'

'I have given up wondering; I am more inclined to sleep,' said Dunn, as Sanderson returned, took his place and opened the book of Huxley's Essays and Lectures, which he had brought down with him. He began to read:

Examine the recently laid egg of some common animal, such as a salamander or a newt. It is a minute spheroid in which the best microscope will reveal nothing but a structureless sac, enclosing a glairy fluid, holding granules in suspension. But strange possibilities lie dormant in that semi-fluid globule. Let a moderate supply of warmth reach its watery cradle, and the plastic matter undergoes changes so rapid and yet so steady and purposelike in their succession, that one can only compare them to those operated by a skilled modeller upon a formless lump of clay. As with an invisible trowel, the mass is divided and subdivided into smaller and smaller portions, until it is reduced to an aggregation of granules not too large to build withal the finest fabrics of the nascent organism. And, then, it is as if a delicate finger traced out the line to be occupied by the spinal column, and moulded the contour of the body; pinching up the head at one end, the tail at the other, and fashioning flank and limb into due salamandrine proportions, in so artistic a way, that, after watching the process hour by hour, one is almost involuntarily possessed by the notion, that some more subtle aid to vision than an achromatic, would show the hidden artist, with his plan before him, striving with skilful manipulation to perfect his work.

'Oh, very nice!' said Hunter appreciatively, as Sanderson closed the book. 'And how much better I like Huxley's hidden artist than your invisible geometry!'

SANDERSON: You can't really compare them. Huxley's artist is a picturesque metaphor—a very striking one—but it is no more. It was a purely imaginary artist, whom he never saw and in whom he didn't believe.

UPWATER: Whereas yours is an actual theory—a sort of neo-vitalism.

SANDERSON: No. I'm sorry. That's exactly what it is *not*.

HUNTER: Much more like Neo-Platonism.

UPWATER: Then what is it? I thought I was following you with some sympathy. A lot of the phenomena in biology *are* impossible to explain in mechanistic terms, and not very easy even with the concepts of modern bio-chemistry. I thought you were saying something like Bertalanffy—that we must develop new concepts for the understanding of living organisms.

SANDERSON: I dare say you must. I should think it very likely. But it is not those I am talking of. Theories like vitalism, or those of organismic biology—are simply thought-models, evolved inside a scientist's head to enable him to account for the phenomena which he observes. Just as mechanism was another and cruder thought-model. They do not amount to a participation of the knower *in* the unconscious thinking that is going on in nature. That is only achieved by contemplating the phenomena themselves in concentrated mental activity, but without at the time thinking *about* them. Then they begin to explain themselves. Then they appear as what they are in time as well as in space. You are talking about substituting one idea for

another; I am talking about widening the faculty and
range of a man's perception; theories *about* what is
observed would be a second stage. I am still at the stage
of observation itself. A very much closer comparison —
indeed more than a comparison — for what I am
saying would be the Goethean morphology. You can
call his 'archetypal plant' an idea or a theory if you
like — as Schiller did when he first heard of it, Schiller
being a good Box and Cox Kantian. But it is a complete
misunderstanding of what Goethe was actually
talking about.

HUNTER: But those who haven't got this widened range
of perception, which you and Goethe are talking
about, have either got to take it on trust or else to
treat it as a theory and try it out experimentally like
any other theory!

SANDERSON: Yes — unless they think it worth while to set
about acquiring it.

UPWATER: You want to make your scientist into a mystic!

SANDERSON: Nonsense! We have talked a good deal about
the difference between the 'aided' and the 'unaided'
senses. If there are other ways of aiding the senses
besides the use of precision instruments, I for one do
not see how science can afford to neglect them.

BRODIE: Ah, it can be acquired can it? I was beginning
to think it was a kind of second-sight, that a few of
us are born with, and most of us without. How do
you set about it?

SANDERSON: It would take a long time to answer that
fully. But in the first place it involves *looking* at the

phenomena open-mindedly, without at that stage obtruding any theoretical cerebration, conscious or unconscious, and letting them speak to you for themselves.

BURGEON: As far as that goes it's the same with a symbol—if it's a genuine one. It is only when you attend to it wholeheartedly instead of speculating on what is behind it that—that you really *reach* what is behind it.

SANDERSON: Take Huxley himself. Of course he knew nothing about the kind of thing I have just been saying, but he was by instinct such a devout naturalist that it seems he was sometimes content simply to sit and *watch* a natural process 'hour by hour', as he says. The result was that not even the 'spectre', not even positivism, in all its nineteenth-century heyday, could prevent him from *almost* seeing with his eyes what is going on in a process of organic growth.

But I am no more called on to give a lecture than Brodie or anyone else here. If you want to follow it up, read Goethe's *Metamorphosis of Plants*, or some of his other scientific writings, or the Introductions to them that Steiner wrote when he was editing them. Or perhaps, for the particular approach I have made (especially as I have harped a bit on projective geometry), you would do better still with Adams and Whicher's *The Plant between Sun and Earth*. I am rather sorry we have got so far away from our principal bone of contention.

BRODIE: What do you say that is?

SANDERSON: Evolution, surely! Look at the time we have spent on it! But it does seem that, unless you first rid yourself of the prevailing obsession that thinking is an activity that stops short at the skin, you will never succeed in reaching a really viable concept of evolution. I mean one which is not open to the objections put by Burgeon and Brodie this morning.

RANGER: Why?

SANDERSON: For the same reason that, if you are a depth-psychologist, you will have to reduce the unconscious and its symbols to bodily processes: because you will go on taking it for granted that consciousness is somehow secondary to material forms. This is the characteristic assumption underlying a particular attitude of mind, which I come up against often enough and which I learnt for the first time yesterday has a name of its own—positivism; it is the assumption on which the whole current picture of evolution is based and therefore the assumption in the light of which all phenomena are interpreted and all experiments conducted. So that any other *kind* of interpretation is ruled out in advance. Burgeon put it jokingly this morning; but it is true enough. Anyone suggesting any other interpretation has this enormous weight to contend with, this colossal inertia of ancient custom. Anything more than a hundred years old is ancient, isn't it, Ranger?

BURGEON: In the world of books, or opinions about books, the age at which senility sets in has now been reduced to about ten.

SANDERSON: Exactly. And *we've* got about two hundred years to contend with. It's like trying to shift a block of granite. Well, I suppose it's pretty much what Galileo's adherents felt about Aristotelianism. And the point is, to keep on trying. Very well then: Now one thing we shall probably agree on is, that ontogenetic development roughly recapitulates phylogenetic evolution.

UPWATER: On the contrary, my friend——

SANDERSON: I said *roughly*. I have read *Embryos and Ancestors*. I simply mean that, in their earlier stages of development, the embryos of the higher phyla do closely resemble those of the lower. I don't see how any unprejudiced person can dispute that phylogenetic evolution and ontogenetic development appear homologous.

UPWATER: If you are going to draw inferences——

SANDERSON: I am not. I drew attention to the homology merely to introduce what I am now going to say. Which is, that you can apply to evolution itself the same method that I have suggested can be applied ontogenetically. If you do so, you arrive, in my opinion, at a convincing picture of the evolution of the mind of man as we know it, just as in the other case you arrived at a convincing picture of the development of his mind in an individual man. I won't argue for it—or not at this stage—I will simply sketch the picture you in fact come to accept. It also seems to me to have a bearing on the relation between evolution, properly so called, and 'history', which was a bone of contention here at one stage.

You come to see this evolution—you cannot help
seeing it—as divided broadly into three periods. I
don't know what I ought to call them; but let me call
the first period 'primeval'. It would cover all the first
part of what Upwater was saying yesterday. In his
view it is the period before man appeared on the scene
at all. In mine it is the period when the forces—if I
may use that neutral word for the moment—which
the human being afterwards came to appropriate for
his thinking faculty, were still engaged in producing,
or evolving, the human *form*.

The second period, which I will call 'pre-historic',
is the one which Burgeon was most concerned with.
It is the period in which *speech* was born, and I
believe he is right in thinking of all development in
that period, whether of man or nature, as having been
largely determined by the whole nature and quality
of language. You have to look back into a time when
words and the thought within them were inseparably
one; and, I think it would also be true to say, when
sound and meaning were still united with one
another in a way we have long lost sight of.

The shaping spirit—spirits—'invisible artists', if you
like—who had been at work on the physical form,
and I mean on its phylogenetic development, now began
to make use of the structure they had created, to
work outward again from it, to reappear, in fact, as the
symbolizing faculty in which Burgeon and his friends
are interested. You cannot really separate the origin
of language from that moment, or that process.

It is only the third period which I would think ought to be called historical. Didn't R. G. Collingwood maintain that all history is the history of thought? I don't know if that is the right way to put it; but I would agree that the historical period, as distinct from the other two, comes into its own precisely as man's thinking begins to detach itself, as 'meaning', from the sounds in which he has to express it. No doubt this was connected also with the origin of writing. Language becomes less and less a duet with nature; more and more a means of communication between man and man. That is, more and more subjective; more and more a mere vehicle for passing to and fro the abstract and personalized experience, the *waking* experiences, which are beginning to characterize humanity. More and more a tool which can be used for severely practical purposes. More and more like what Dunn thinks language is now and, I suppose, thinks it always has been.

As I see it, this is the period in which we are now living and I would say we are still pretty near the beginning of it. No doubt that was why it was able to take such a big leap forward at the time of the scientific revolution.

UPWATER: Is that all? I thought we were in for something much more exciting. There may be something in what you say about your last two periods. At least any evidence there may be for it can be properly tested by scientific methods, so that it will be either rejected or established. But as to the first period, which I understand is limited to physical evolution, you can have no evidence at all. You seem to agree that the physical body of *homo sapiens* had to evolve into a suitable organism before it could start speaking and thinking. But then you go on to assert that this organism was somehow 'geometrized' into being out of nothing.

SANDERSON: Not out of nothing.

UPWATER: Well, out of space or something. It is a pretty and poetical notion. But you must forgive us for being satisfied that in fact *homo sapiens* was evolved through the rough and tumble of natural selection— a process which we still see quite clearly going on all round us. What is wrong with the simpler hypothesis?

SANDERSON: Well, you know, we have been hearing a good deal that is wrong with it. Even if we take them both as no more than speculations, I think it can still be argued that my account fits the facts better. In the first place there is this very fact with which I started—the broadly homologous relation between phylogenetic and ontogenetic process. We must both accept it as a fact at the hands of embryology. But then, it seems to me, *you* have to accept the fact as an unaccountable freak of nature; whereas it follows inevitably from my view.

UPWATER: But how?

SANDERSON: Because both are the work of the same 'invisible artist', as Huxley put it. Because both are instances of the way in which a physical organism emerges from a spiritual background and becomes in its turn capable of spiritual activity.

Then again it has been strongly suggested that you
have no satisfactory place for reason in your system,
and therefore no safe ground for asserting that what
you say is true. At most you can throw out some casual
suggestions about mind having been 'potential' in
the early stages of evolution. But I and those who
think with me are not satisfied with this sort of verbal
salvation. As I said, if we find mind or reason
appearing somewhere for the first time, we think it
is the task of science to inquire more exactly into its
provenance.

And here again, I submit, we get a lot of help
from relating the phylogenetic and the ontogenetic
approaches. For us, the relation between mind and
body which characterized the first period of evolution,
has not simply disappeared. It is still there. And so
indeed is the relation that obtained in the second
period. But then we do not think of man as simply
a brain on legs.

BURROWS: Who does?

SANDERSON: I rather suspect Dunn does. And I'm not
quite sure about Upwater. Anyway we think of him
as in all respects—physically as well as spiritually—a
threefold organism. He is not always thinking and he
is not always awake. He thinks and feels and wills;
and he wakes and dreams and sleeps. Even while he
is awake, he is still a sleeper in his will. What does he
know of his volitional process—except its results?—
and he is a dreamer in his feeling life. It is only in his
thinking that he is really awake. And all this is

reflected in the form itself of his physical structure. If, that is, you really *look* at it as Huxley really looked at his egg. He has his brain, for his waking life, swelled out into a bubble in his head, but radiating in the form of nerves through the whole organism. In all this, but especially in the head, he can be psychically active, because he is physically passive. He has, at the other pole, his motor organism—limbs and metabolism—which also reaches up into the head, in the form and function of mouth and lower jaw. And between the two poles his heart and chest, his breathing and his blood circulation—which also permeate the whole body, but are focused in his heart and lungs.

We say that, when he is asleep—and also, even during the day, in his unconscious, from which his impulses of will spring so unaccountably—his relation to the spirit is still that of the first period. In his dreaming, and, in the half-conscious goings-on of his emotional life, he is still really living in the second period. It is only when he is wide-awake, and actually thinking and perceiving that he is wholly up to date.

DUNN: So what?

SANDERSON: So a good deal. But I dare say you have had enough of it, and it's time I gave way to someone else.

BURGEON: I haven't.

HUNTER: I am quite ready for some more.

BRODIE: I think you'll have to go on, Sanderson. You can't just leave your threefold man hanging in the air like that.

SANDERSON: Very well. I'll go on trying. The first answer I should offer to Dunn is, I think, this. If we see right, the whole being of man, both his spiritual constitution and his physical structure, seems to be designed as an answer to precisely that gulf between the conscious and the unconscious, which has been giving us so much trouble. Or, if you like, as a potential means of overcoming it.

HUNTER: You want to get Box and Cox into a double bed.

SANDERSON: Yes. Except that a bed is a place for sleeping in, and I want them to be awake. Again, if we are right, there are other ways of bringing the unconscious part of us into the light of consciousness besides psycho-analysis, however well adapted that may be to pathological cases. It is possible, though it is a pretty strenuous business, to bring your willing *systematically* into your thinking. But you cannot do it, if you insist on leaving out feeling; because feeling is the field where the tension between the two poles, of conscious and unconscious, in fact operates.

This of course is where we come up against the present habit of scientific thought. It is right that we should. One of the first principles of science is that all feeling must be ruled out, where scientific investigation is concerned. But then it is always assumed that, when one speaks of 'feeling', one means subjective feelings—wishes and so forth—by which one's thinking is unconsciously influenced. But that is not what I mean at all. There is such a thing as objective

feeling, which can be used as a means to clearer
thinking and deeper perception.

BURGEON: Any competent poet or painter knows that.

SANDERSON: Yes, but his object is not scientific
investigation. What I am trying to put is that, if a
man deliberately *strengthens* his thinking in the sort
of way I am suggesting—by uniting with it the natural
energy of his feeling and willing—he begins to
penetrate, with consciousness, into those other parts
of his organism where the older relation between
man and nature still persists. He becomes aware of
what is going on at the normally unconscious pole,
able to observe it, and in this way he gains direct access
to the past, that is, to the primeval period when that
relation prevailed. You can say he re-enacts it in
conscious experience; or you can say that he actually
observes the past, instead of having to *infer* it in his
fancy from the present. They are two different ways
of putting the same thing.

UPWATER: You don't seem to like inference. If I understand
you rightly, it boils down to this. By concentrating
introspectively on our own natural instincts we can
build up some kind of picture of the less conscious
element in man's present relation to nature, and we
can then take the enormous jump of saying that this
is what the primeval relation was like! If you had any
acquaintance with the actual practice of zoology, you
would not, I am sure, make such an extraordinary
suggestion. It is one thing to argue, from your
philosophical armchair, about the limitations of all

knowledge-by-inference, but it is quite another thing to move about in it all. I agree, of course, that in the last analysis, no theory about the past can be *experimentally* verified. That is self-evident. But if you were at all familiar with the steadily accumulating mass of detailed observations on which modern theories of biological evolution are based, the racks and racks of tabulated quantitative measurements, the probings, the fierce attacks to which every hypothesis is subjected before it is established, you would begin to talk very differently. You would at least accept, as every reasonable man does, the broad picture of evolution as it stands today, instead of ransacking your brains for some fantasy of your own to substitute for it.

SANDERSON: I am perhaps a *little* more familiar with all that than you suppose. But I don't dispute that, if I knew more, I should be even more impressed than I am at present with the profusion of accurate observations and the conscientious records kept of them. It is not the observations themselves that I quarrel with. What I do say is, that the field over which your observations have so far been conducted is arbitrarily restricted and the class of conclusions to be drawn from those that *are* conducted, is determined in advance, by the central assumption from which you start. Further, that this assumption does not itself arise from the observations, but is arbitrarily imposed on them.

UPWATER: Since the conclusions cover the observable facts, why is there any need to open the door to more recondite ones?

SANDERSON: But *do* they cover them? The observable facts are—the whole of nature as we see it around us today. Isn't there a tendency to select from that whole those facts that happen to fit the theory most comfortably? Are you really satisfied that, if you look round at nature, without preconceptions, with a really unprejudiced eye, there is nothing there that is not explainable by chance mutations and natural selection?

Obviously we can't go into a lot of detail. It wouldn't be fair on the others. We might some time discuss it privately if you care to.

UPWATER: Not if you are merely going to put up a few special freaks of nature and challenge me to account for them by natural selection. I am tired of that game.

SANDERSON: I don't find that they are so few. And really I think the boot is on the other leg. I have very much in mind what Burrows said (it was about Dunn's contention that we have no private experience)— that you can prove an awful lot, to your own satisfaction at any rate, if you confine yourself to the simplest end of the scale of the phenomena you are dealing with. We don't hear very much about the giraffe's neck these days, but I am getting very tired of those 'stick-like' insects, which fit in so nicely with Darwin. You don't like freaks, so we'll leave out alternate generation, or the life-history of the Gordius-fly described by Agassiz, or the numerous examples of complex symbiosis and the like that in our own time Grant Watson has described so delicately in his books. No doubt they're at the *other* end of the scale. But I should have thought there was quite enough round about the middle of the scale to rule out natural selection and adaptive radiation as the *principal* factor in their provenance—enough for anyone who is not strongly biased in its favour to start with. I have never understood, for one thing, how you get round the fact that the end-product so often has a character obviously out of line with the mindless process said to have produced it. So that it is really impossible to imagine how any intermediate stage could have had any survival-value—the colonial and matrimonial arrangements of bees, for instance; or the delicate interdependence between flowers and the insects that fertilize them.

UPWATER: You people always leave out the infinite amount of time, running into billions of years, over which it all went on.

SANDERSON: Yes, but unlimited time doesn't render conceivable an inherently inconceivable sequence of events. Are you going to force me to bring out those monkeys and their typewriters?

BURGEON: What does he mean?

SANDERSON: It has been suggested that, if you provided a colony of monkeys with typewriters to play with, then, provided you allowed them infinite time, there would be nothing to prevent them producing by accident the complete works of Shakespeare. In the same way, if you allow it enough billions of years, there was nothing to prevent natural selection from producing by accident the elaborate organization and apparent design in, for instance, a community of ants or bees.

I am supposed to be saying what I think, rather than criticizing any other view, so I will keep down criticism to a minimum. But it can't be altogether avoided.

BURGEON: Naturally. As between heresy and orthodoxy the burden of proof is on heresy, so it *must* try to show where orthodoxy is wrong. Whereas orthodoxy can rely comfortably on the fact that it is orthodox.

HUNTER: Until it is attacked.

SANDERSON: Yes. Until it is attacked. But hasn't the attack on the central fortress of evolutionary orthodoxy been delivered here already—and much better than I could have done it?

UPWATER: A lot of things have been said. What do you mean by the central fortress?

SANDERSON: I don't mean the theory of natural selection. I have no doubt that was an important physical factor; I only think its significance has been exaggerated. I don't mean the theory that the human form evolved from the animal form. Physically speaking, I think it largely did. I mean the assumption that organic matter evolved from inorganic, and that the phenomenon of solidity preceded the phenomenon of life. In my view these are both not only pure assumptions but also highly arbitrary ones.

RANGER: But haven't the relative ages of rocks and fossils and things been scientifically determined by all sorts of evidence—radio-activity, carbon 14, and so on?

SANDERSON: Yes. But the assumptions come first. And the evidence is then interpreted in the light of them. If we started with different assumptions, we should quickly find different interpretations. I've no doubt you could infer all sorts of immemorial things about the age of a human liver, if you had the fixed idea that it was a piece of inorganic matter, and if you did not happen to know that seventy or eighty years ago it just wasn't there!

UPWATER: That's rather absurd.

SANDERSON: It isn't only absurd. It's impossible. I am only struggling to make my meaning clear with the help of an impossible illustration.

HUNTER: As many good men have done before you.

BURGEON: A metaphor may be all the better for being absurd.

SANDERSON: The central fortress, then, is the 'primeval' inorganic solidity of the earth. It has already been attacked here—at considerable length. On the one hand it is said that the earth as we know it, including its 'secondary' quality of solidity, is a construct of the human brain; and, thus, that brain and solidity are correlatives; on the other hand it is assumed that the earth as we know it was there for billions of years before there was a human, or any other brain in existence. You heard the argument. Perhaps you have an answer to it. I haven't. If the argument is right, the whole thing is a preposterous extrapolation, an impossible fancy. Every bit as impossible as my fancy just now about a theoretically inorganic liver.

And the fact that it is accepted by millions does not, you know, make it any less impossible.

Of course there are other grounds for abandoning it, but I should have thought one unanswerable one was enough. Anyway I don't think it's for me to go on arguing it. Sooner or later people will make up their minds whether it is to be abandoned or not. All I will say is, that once you *have* abandoned it, you become for the first time able to observe the phenomena of nature in a really unprejudiced way. And if you really *look*, in that way, at a simple phenomenon like, say, a flower and the butterfly hovering over it, it will really tell you of itself that it is not something that arose through the interplay of discrete physical units, but the material manifestation of an immaterial unity from which both flower and butterfly have sprung. An invisible 'common ancestor', if you like.

Incidentally, Upwater, haven't you got to admit that the common ancestor of man and the primates— and indeed of a good many of the lower phyla also— *is* pretty elusive? One after another surviving, or excavated, genus turns out to be an end-product of adaptation instead of a step in the main line of descent. You are getting a hypothetical 'tree' of descent which is all branches and no trunk. And then, because you insist that the higher forms had no existence of *any* sort until they appeared in physical form, you have to knock together some hypothesis like 'neoteny' to account for it.

But I have dropped into argument and criticism again. The short point is that, *if* you can bring yourself to admit the possibility that the whole earth was a living organism to start with, there is no reason to presume that life and consciousness, in varied forms, was not present while it was still in a liquid state and, before that, in its gaseous or aery condition.

UPWATER: Oh, this is nonsense.

SANDERSON: But *why?* When it is the opposite assumption that is contrary to all experience. The assumption that matter first evolved to the requisite complexity and then became capable of sustaining, and somehow gave rise to, life? Possibly life *could* be produced in that order. The biochemists are trying to do it and may succeed for all I know. But what we actually observe happening round us is in fact always in the opposite order. Liquidity precedes solidity and solidity only becomes absolute with death. Life comes first and gives rise to dead matter. The geology of the Secondary Period shouts it aloud at us. How much of inorganic matter is in fact organic debris?

You will find there is nothing in what I am saying that runs counter to the observed facts. It is only the prior assumptions that we question, and the theories fathered by them. On the contrary, if you would once try the experiment of giving us the benefit of the doubt, I believe you would be surprised how many things would fall into place and how many awkwardnesses would disappear.

You show us how a new type appears and in course of time radiates into a beautifully varied harmony of adaptation to its environment. All you are really being asked to do is to keep an open mind as to where the new type comes from in the first place; and to the whole way an organism is inserted in its environment. Surely it is a very arbitrary methodological restriction which prescribes that the organism must always be conceived of as cut off from its environment, that the *interdependence* of object and environment is of only secondary importance, and that the object's evolution must be treated primarily as a closed causal system!

I would go further than that myself and say that such a restriction is not only arbitrary, but also crudely anthropomorphic! For it is just of the human being himself, and only of the human being—and then only since the seventeenth century—that this cutting off from environment is in fact characteristic. But I won't press that, in case it takes us back over old ground.

What's the time? Good heavens, I must obviously finish. It boils down to this. *You* say that man and his mind had no existence at all until he grew up somehow on a solid earth that had existed for billions of years beforehand. I say that it is a mistake to fancy a solid earth—or a material earth of any description that we should recognize—before physical man was in existence with a physical brain. I say, further, that a great deal of the evolution which you depict in terms of a physical model was in fact an immaterial process. Even the oldest *fossils*, as you know, are of organisms already highly evolved.

BURGEON: There is still the question of when man *did* appear.

SANDERSON: I say he was there, in his unconscious, from the beginning. And I say it is just that beginning to which those paradise-myths, which as we have heard are found all over the earth, point back; that they are a dim recollection in tradition of the state of affairs that obtained before his more conscious life had developed. If your picture is right, one would expect the recollection and the tradition to contain some trace of it. Why don't they? Why do none of the myths anywhere symbolize this ascent of man from animal, which you say covers all the facts? And how do you explain, even with the dubious assistance of 'animism', the account which they do give, not only of man himself, but of nature also—and of a very different ancestral relation between the two from the one we know?

BURGEON: That's true enough; they commonly speak of an intimate relation between man and the other creatures, which has somehow been lost. 'In those days men and beasts could still talk to each other'—and so on. Moreover, the folk-tales that tell of such intercourse, even when they are not recognizably paradise-narratives, often have a paradisal aura about them,

SANDERSON: Yes. Because they are traditions of the common origin of man and nature in a world which was not yet material. It was the descent from this condition into physical incarnation which made that separate existence possible. And there is no dispute that the plants and animals *descended* first. That, as I see it, is the truth of which the 'neoteny' theory is a caricature. And even the accepted neo-Darwinian picture of evolution is much more like a caricature than a contradiction of the underlying facts. If you are going to ask why it all became competitive and a struggle for existence arose, one would have to go into the vexed question of the origin of evil. It seems to me we shall have to leave that out—though it is absurd, from another point of view, to do so. But until there is at least *some* measure of agreement about *what* happened, it seems rather a waste of time to start talking about *why* it happened. And I doubt if we are even in sight of such an agreement.

UPWATER: I'm afraid not.

BURGEON: We certainly shan't arrive at it between now and dinner.

SANDERSON: I don't think we shall arrive at it at all. The idea, as I understood it, was that we should at least hear what the other fellow has to say; and I have been trying this evening to do my bit. I have been endeavouring like Jeeves, to give satisfaction! Perhaps Jeeves comes to mind because I have just heard Burgeon mention dinner. Meanwhile, we can at least agree on one point; and that is—that it is high time we went off to get some.

THIRD DAY

THE NEXT DAY began gloomily. In the Sunday paper delivered to us during breakfast the news from behind the Iron Curtain had grown more menacing. The threat of rain, which had kept us indoors the previous afternoon, had never materialized, but neither had the sky grown any clearer. The clouds were lower now and it was growing uncomfortably hot; but hot as it was, it was clearly not a morning for another session in the garden. Our last session it must be; for several of the party had to leave soon after lunch.

As soon as we were all assembled in the sitting-room, and before I had switched on the tape-recorder, Dunn announced that he would like to lead off. We agreed to this and he began as follows:

DUNN: I have been wondering since yesterday evening if I may perhaps have been a little lazy. It may be I ought to have said more at an earlier stage; but in any case if I say it now, it may possibly avoid our being led up a false trail and wasting a lot of time.

On Friday evening the question was raised, and quickly dropped again, of what is meant by a scientific hypothesis. If I remember right, Hunter asked Upwater if, by an established theory, he meant one which is proved to be true and may turn out to be false. And Upwater agreed rather reluctantly with that way of putting it. But there was no general agreement and I myself registered my dissent.

In my opinion not only everything Sanderson said yesterday, but also the whole of the dialogue between Burgeon and Brodie was misconceived. It was all founded on a total misunderstanding of what any scientific inference or hypothesis is intended to be or can be. It is a misunderstanding that is very common among those who are neither themselves actively concerned with actual scientific research nor in constant touch with the people who are. Very shortly it consists in putting things the wrong way round. The assumption from which these non-scientific critics of science start is, that 'truth' is something to be looked for somewhere *behind* or beyond experience. Observations, they think, are made, then a theory is formed to 'explain' them; and then experiments are conducted with the object of proving the truth or untruth of the theory. This is quite wrong. It may once have been what was meant by scientific research, but it is not what is meant today. Any scientist worth his salt knows that in the real business of research it is exactly the other way round. Theories or inferences are not evolved to explain observations or the results of experiment, and experiments are not made in order to decide whether a particular theory is 'true' or not. The function of a theory is not to give us something called 'knowledge' about something called 'truth', which lies in some mysterious way behind the phenomena. Knowledge is *in* experience, not behind or beyond it. Theories are nothing; they are expendable the moment they cease to fit, and therefore to help, experience. What theories do is, first, to enable the scientist to predict events and, second, to enable him to arrange effective further experiments. They take the *form* of statements of fact (statements about so-called 'laws' of nature and so forth) because that is the only way language has yet found of expressing them. But functionally they are not statements of fact at all. That is why it is safer to call them 'models' than theories. Because no one doubts that a model is expendable as soon as it has served its purpose and no one is in any danger of falsely identifying a mental model, which he or anyone else has mocked up for practical purposes, with actual experience; or with 'knowledge', which is the same thing.

BURROWS: This is Ranger's argument again, isn't it? It *works!*

DUNN: No. I think Ranger was really arguing that the models must exist, and the theories must be 'true', *because* they work technologically. But that way of putting it is really only fanciful. The working *is* the truth; and the rest—theories, models and anything of the sort—is mere expendable cerebration.

BRODIE: That is pretty much how any of my colleagues who bother to think about it at all would put it. Only they would not put it so clearly. Do you not find something unsatisfactory in it?

DUNN: My point is, that if we are to go on listening to Sanderson's theories, we should at least do so with our eyes open and not pretend to ourselves that they have anything to do with science.

BURGEON: But does not the same objection apply to Upwater's?

DUNN: Upwater's? Why?

BURGEON: Because everything that is actually in the *past* does lie beyond our experience. What becomes of the theory of natural selection then, or any other theory of evolution?

DUNN: It is quite different. The events that happened were *within* the experience of those living at the time.

HUNTER: I see no justification whatever for that distinction. You can't have it both ways, you know. Either you are saying that all knowledge lies in, and not beyond, the experience of the knower, or you are not. If you *are* saying it, it seems to me Burgeon is right and, quite apart from evolution, there is no such thing as even *history.* Or at least, from the point of view of what you call science, no particular piece of history is either true or untrue, because it is beyond our experience.

DUNN: Well, perhaps by the strictest standards we should have to say so.

BURGEON: That is just what I object to. You people uphold the strictest standards with a great flourish against everyone else. But you are quite ready to drop them the moment they become inconvenient to you. We are told that scientific theories are reliable in quite a different way from any others, because they are always tested by prediction and experiment. And then, hey presto, the prestige of this reliability is transferred to a whole bunch of sciences from which both prediction and experiment are ruled out *a priori*, whether because they deal with past time, or because they deal with fantastically distant space, or for some other reason. We are told, moreover, that the theories of science are not important anyway, if we are on the look-out for truth or knowledge, because they are only expendable models. And hey presto, this new definition of a theory, which places every theory beyond criticism, is transferred, as a kind of numinous aura, to any number of theories, which are quite open and unabashed *theories* in the good old sense we are all familiar with. I don't know how scientists talk to each other in their laboratories, but you know perfectly well that, whenever they come before the public, they talk in the ordinary way about what they know and what they don't know, and what they believe things are actually like behind the phenomena. If you have any doubt about it, just have a look at *The Times* Special Number on the Tercentenary of the Royal Society, July 19th, 1961.

HUNTER: It seems to me there are two points. First, as to the sciences, like physics, which *can* be proved by prediction and experiment. No one questions that important results are obtained by a willingness to treat every theory simply as an expendable model. Point one, therefore: does that rule out the possibility of our also arriving at some actual truth by the use of reason and inference? Point two: if it doesn't, then, as to the other sciences, which *cannot* test their theories by either prediction or experiment, how do we distinguish a theory that is entitled to be called 'scientific' from any other sort of theory? Of course, if the 'expendable model' principle *does* rule out the possibility of arriving at truth by reason and inference, we need not bother ourselves with those other sciences because they would not be sciences at all, as we have now defined the term.

SANDERSON: I have learnt a great deal during these two days and one of the things I have learnt is, that it is not altogether difficult to make modern science look rather silly. But somehow, though I see the force of the arguments, at the back of my mind I remain unimpressed by them, or rather, not unimpressed, unmoved. No doubt scientists—especially when they are making public pronouncements—do from time to time say some very foolish things. But the fact remains, for me at any rate, that the scientific revolution was *the* great achievement of the human spirit. It was an incalculable advance on anything that had gone before, when scientists finally gave up inferring to spiritual and metaphysical causes and began looking to the phenomena to explain themselves. It brought to us all, not only a new freedom, but a new *kind* of freedom altogether. If only they had kept it up! My quarrel with modern science, as it has actually developed, is not for rejecting theory and contenting itself with the phenomena; it is for *not* doing so. I do not quarrel with scientists for refusing to try to penetrate to a realm beyond experience; I quarrel with them for spending most of their time in just that realm.

Brodie's two quotations from Galileo yesterday were a revelation to me. The first one, where he said that error may lurk unnoticed in the hypotheses of reason but 'a discovery of sense cannot err', was the pure principle of science, as I understand it. It was science itself speaking with its own new voice. The second one, where he positively gloried in the fact that reason does violence to the evidence of the senses and that men can be taught to prefer the hypotheses of reason to the sense-experience which contradicts them, represents an aberration from the true principle, which seems to have begun almost as soon as the principle itself was discovered. The 'exhibition dialogue', as someone has called it, rubbed in how far that contradiction has been carried since. Surely that way of looking at it was a backsliding into the very mire from which the scientific revolution had just rescued us! It's as if we had started picking up from the ground the broken fetters we had only just struck off, and forging them into new ones of exactly the same kind. For abstract theories, or rather any so-called 'laws' of nature, *are* metaphysical causes, and, whether we take them literally or treat them as 'models', if we spend most of our time paddling about among them, we *are* trying to get beyond experience, instead of staying in it. For me, that is one of the good things about space-travel. It will at least be *aiming* at first-hand experience.

I agree absolutely with Dunn, therefore, that knowledge lies *in* experience, not beyond it. The only thing I object to is his making *me* his scapegoat for the very sin I particularly abhor.

DUNN: I really don't see what better example there could be of theorizing, in the old sense, than the sort of things you were saying yesterday evening.

SANDERSON: You are mistaken. I took a good deal of trouble to insist—and I am sure the tape-recorder would bear me out if you played it back—that what I was describing was not inferred theoretically, but experienced.

DUNN: You may have said so, because you don't like the *word* theory. But what else was it in fact? You were telling us about, or, rather actually *describing*, a whole class of events alleged to occur in some imperceptible realm which precedes sense-experience ——

SANDERSON: Not imperceptible. On the contrary, I expressly said it was perceptible.

HUNTER: He did say that, when he was talking about children and about his geometrizing space, or geometrizing ether. But he went on to give his own account of evolution. Supposing he is right—and I don't know on what authority he says it—perhaps he can go into that later—but supposing he is right about space, I still don't see how it helps him with time; or how he is any better off there than Upwater. You, or your friends, Sanderson, may be able to see, or to perceive in some other way, goings on in space that ordinary people can't see. But you'll not maintain that you can see the past?

SANDERSON: As a matter of fact I'm afraid I shall. Or at least that we *could* do so. Indeed I've suggested it already. I know it sounds startling. But it also seems to me somehow natural and inevitable. You yourself have just pointed out that we can never have a science of evolution or even of history—not, that is, as Dunn or Brodie's friends understand 'science'—on any other terms.

HUNTER: It doesn't follow that we can have one at all. But you must have a very remarkable theory of perception. Perhaps we ought to hear some more about it.

SANDERSON: I suppose so—yes.

BRODIE: You don't sound very enthusiastic over it.

SANDERSON: I shall have to confess that I am worried by one of the arguments Dunn put up yesterday. He insisted that it is a mistake to treat perception as though it were compounded of sense-impressions. He pointed out that we never experience a sense-impression 'neat', as it were, and that, if we try to go behind our perceptions as they are actually given, we are doing the very thing I have just agreed we shouldn't do—that is, pretending we can go behind experience. It sounded convincing, and yet it seems obvious to me that perception *is* made up of sense-impressions—as Galileo and most other people seem to have assumed.

HUNTER: I shouldn't worry too much about that. When we talk about a 'theory of perception', we may mean two very different things. We may mean the sort of thing Ranger and Upwater have in mind, that is, a theory of how the brain and the sense-organs function and so forth. That is a scientific inquiry, and the rules for scientific inquiry (whatever they are) are properly applied to it.

But we may also mean the kind of thing Dunn himself does. That is, inquiring into the question how we ever come to perceive and conceive such an object as a brain, or any other object, at all. That question obviously cannot be answered simply by *another* scientific inquiry into the functioning of the brain and senses. We touched on this yesterday. We must already have perceived before we can start examining. The thing we are examining had first been made available. How? We perceive a bit of brain-tissue lying on a dissecting-table and we form theories about how the brain enables perceiving and thinking and so on. But such questions as, for instance, whether we can *rely* on the perception we started with, or whether all perception is some kind of hoax or illusion, or whether it is nonsense to entertain speculations about its being a hoax or illusion, obviously cannot be answered by theories inferred *from* that very perception. Inquiries of this second kind are not scientific at all. They are analytical. In that sense *every* critic of science must be 'non-scientific'. Science, or knowledge, is one thing. Theories about the *nature* of science or knowledge are another. And quite different rules must apply to them.

DUNN: I do not agree.

HUNTER: Surely you must! You yourself are an 'analyst'. Your book reaches the conclusion that the only knowledge we can have is empirical, and that our starting-point must be the normal perceptions of normal people. But *that statement* itself, and the argument leading up to it, is not empirical. When did you last see or smell or taste a tautology, for instance? Your own argument is not based on perception; it is *about* perception. How then can you insist that all other people who inquire into the same subject-matter must start from the point where you leave off?

DUNN: That is a cheap gibe.

SANDERSON: I don't see why, but I'll leave you to settle it between you. As far as I am concerned, if we think about (which I suppose is analysing) our own experience in perception—that is, the way we normally see the world—we *must*, I feel, admit that it is already an elaborate compound of thoughts and sense-impressions, or concepts and percepts. I just don't see any alternative. Anyway I must start from that assumption, and a good deal has been said about it already—especially by Burgeon.

DUNN: As long as you agree that it is a bare assumption.

BURGEON: It isn't 'bare' at all. It's not a matter of experience; but neither, as Hunter has pointed out, is it a hypothesis. It's a conclusion compelled by reason as soon as we bring reason to bear on our own immediate experience in thinking and perceiving. Your argument seems to be that we cannot, or must not, distinguish the conceptual element in what you call normal perception from the perceptual element, because we never have them separate in practice, because we never experience a bare sense-impression before it has been built up into the complex perception of some object. Supposing your premiss is correct (I'm not sure that it is), the conclusion doesn't follow for a moment. The rule that you must not distinguish where you carmot divide, is not simply a mistake. It's a howler. For that is exactly what reason does do. It is the very thing it is *there* to do!

HUNTER: It has just occurred to me that perhaps the converse of the howler—the belief that you *must* divide, in order to distinguish—may be what lies at the back of that persistent quest for smaller and smaller units, which was mentioned, and which seems to have become a sort of golden rule for scientific investigation, though I could never understand why.

BURGEON: Nor could I. Only a fool has to take a house to pieces to find out that it is made of bricks; and only a bigger fool gets so interested in the bricks, when he has done so, that he says they built the house. As to why we should insist on confining ourselves to it for ever, and remain incapable of conceiving the bare possibility of any other approach—I doubt if there *is* any explanation—except possibly the chicken and the chalk line.

RANGER: What chicken?

BURGEON: If you hold a chicken's head to the ground and draw a chalk line down the middle of its beak and on along the ground in front of it, and then go away, the chicken will remain rooted to the spot, until you come and release it. At least I have been told so. I've never tried it!

SANDERSON: You've started girding again, Burgeon! Can't you stop it? That just isn't true of modern biology as a whole. Alongside the genes and chromosomes, all sorts of fascinating field-studies are going on of living plants and animals and their habitats.

Well, anyway, I start from the assumption that perception, as we know it, normal perception, proves on analysis to be composed of two distinct elements, one of which is conceptual and the other perceptual. We are usually unaware of the conceptual ingredient in the moment of perception. In other words the thinking in it is unconscious. But just because it *is*, nevertheless, thinking—and thinking, as Hunter has said, is essentially 'my act', it follows that we do not, as is commonly assumed, confront the world as detached spectators, when we perceive it, but actively participate in its being with our own being.

RANGER: Do you mean we make it what it is by the way we think about it?

SANDERSON: No. That is more like what Upwater—or the people he was referring to on Friday night—say, the people who talk about nature as a 'construct'. The thinking I am talking about, the thinking that becomes an element in perception, is not *about* our perceptions, it is *in* them. And therefore it is as much in the world we perceive as it is in our perceiving selves.

RANGER: I don't get it.

The day had by now grown almost unbearably hot and airless and the atmosphere in our little room was quite stifling, even though we had the door and all the windows wide open. Most of us already had our ties off and our shirts open and Hunter now got up and took his coat off, an example which Upwater quickly followed.

SANDERSON: Maybe it's because, when I say 'thinking', you assume I mean the kind of thinking of which we are ordinarily conscious, and that already has a tincture of sense-impression in it. That is why we have the illusion that it is going on 'inside' us; whereas in fact it is the sense impressions that are inside us. Remember I am distinguishing what cannot in normal experience be divided. I am talking about the pure concept.

DUNN: *Whose* pure concept?

HUNTER: You ought to know that that is a question that cannot be asked. My concept of a triangle and your concept of a triangle are not two concepts, which are exact replicas of each other. They are one and the same concept. 'I said it very loud and clear: I went and shouted in your ear—' but it's no use of course.

SANDERSON: And yet, if it were not so, we should not all be living in one world, but each in a private world of his own. Which is the very privilege Dunn denies us!

HUNTER: Is it too hot to go on?

RANGER (*mopping his brow with his handkerchief*): You seem to be turning everything upside down. It is the world we *perceive* that is the same for all of us, surely; and our *thoughts* that are private and personal.

SANDERSON: Yes. And it is the thinking *in* the perceiving that makes it one, objective world for all of us. There is nothing more private than a *mere* percept. It may be that we should distinguish it from other kinds of sensation, or even that we ought not to call it a sensation. But it is obviously much more like a sensation than a thing; it is more like a stomach-ache than it is like an external object common to ourselves and others. The concept apart, each one of us sees only his own private cardboard box, and its very shape depends on where he happens to be standing.

BURGEON: Exactly. Therefore it is only people living in the same period and, broadly speaking, in the same community, who inhabit the same world. People living in other periods, or even at the same period but in a totally different community, do not inhabit the same world about which they have different ideas, they inhabit different worlds altogether.

SANDERSON: I don't know that I would go quite as far as that, unless you are using the word 'world' only in a metaphorical sense. There is also the part of the world of which they are collectively unconscious—a pretty extensive part by all accounts.

BURROWS: And what follows from all this?

SANDERSON: Look! You yourself were talking yesterday about the possibility of bringing unconscious processes up to the surface of consciousness; and you said it was the most important discovery science had yet made. You were thinking mainly about memories and emotions, I imagine. My point is that there is the same possibility for thinking. If you systematically strengthen your thinking, so that you gradually become aware not only of the result of it, but of the positive act of thinking itself, you do just that. You become aware of a conceptual area which was previously unconscious. And by doing that, if my theory of perception is correct, you extend the whole depth and range of your perceptions themselves. You begin in fact to perceive parts of the world of which you were previously unaware. You can call it 'controlled clairvoyance', if you like, though it is a word with misleading associations. The point is that, whatever it ought to be called, it is not theorizing. Perception is not theory; it is the subject-matter to which theory is afterwards applied. You can theorize, if you want to, about extended or clairvoyant perceptions, just as you can about so-called 'normal' ones, but they are not themselves theories.

UPWATER: Why throw in a contemptuous 'so-called' before the word 'normal'?

SANDERSON: I suppose I was thinking of what Burgeon said about different perceptions being 'normal' for different periods and different communities—'collective representations', as I believe they have been called. Perhaps I also had in mind something that occurred to me, while you were speaking to us on Friday. If people say that the world we perceive is a 'construct' of our brains, they are saying, in effect, that it results from an inveterate *habit* of thought. Why does it never occur to them that a habit is something you can overcome, if you set about it with enough energy?

BURROWS: Go back to what you were saying about a transition from unconscious to conscious thinking. Can you make it any clearer?

SANDERSON: I'll try. In general I would say that the mind is related to thought in something the same way as the eye is related to light. How much of the light I make, as it were, my own, depends on how much looking I do. In something the same way, how much thought I make my own depends on how much thinking I do. I do not create the thoughts I think any more than I create light. Thinking becomes conscious in me to the extent that I make it my act. Therefore, by extending the range and depth of this activity, I render conscious, thoughts which were previously unconscious. And if I do this with the thoughts which are already inherent in my perception, I render that perception also more conscious and may increase its range and depth.

What I am trying to convey (just how successfully I don't know) is, that a systematic strengthening of our thinking is quite a different proposition from thinking more and more thoughts of the old habitual kind. Just as observing with the help of precision instruments was quite a different proposition from piling up more and more observations of the old unaided kind. The strengthening leads to a different *kind* of thinking.

BURROWS: Can you tell us how it differs from the ordinary kind?

SANDERSON: You are working me pretty hard!

HUNTER: Well, don't go on if you don't want to. There are plenty of other things to talk about.

SANDERSON: Of course I want to. Can I put it this way? When I say 'ordinary thinking', I don't of course mean slovenly or illogical thinking; it can be as acute as you like—for instance the mathematical thinking I was talking of yesterday—only we agreed to call it 'geometrizing'. Ordinary thinking, as I tried to say yesterday, is a sort of reflection back from the brain, after its formation is completed. I agree with Dunn that it is in practice inextricable from sense-impressions. Let me call it 'sense-bound' for short. By strengthening it, you lead it out into the concrete, sense-free thinking which is engaged in *forming* the brain, and indeed the other parts of our organism, and of all organisms. Putting it rather crudely you could say it expands from inside the brain to outside it.

HUNTER: Won't do. You said yesterday that it only entered the brain and became conscious after it had *finished* forming it.

SANDERSON: I am doing the best I can on a very difficult wicket. And I dare say I am not making a very good job of it. You'll have no difficulty in bowling me out with your Box-and-Coxers, if you stick to them. It's a paradox, if you like. But then almost everything to do with thinking is a paradox. Even the simple concept of causality, for example.

BRODIE: How do you make that out?

SANDERSON: Does an effect follow its cause in time, or is it simultaneous with it?

BRODIE: It follows; otherwise it wouldn't *be* an effect.

SANDERSON: I know it wouldn't. Then what happens in the instant of time that elapses between cause and effect? Alternatively, if we say they are simultaneous, how do we distinguish an effect from a cause?

BRODIE: Aha!

SANDERSON: I did suggest, you know, Hunter, when I went on to talk of evolution, that it involves revising our concept of time as well as our concept of space. I even spoke of an older relation between man and nature, which in one sense is finished with but in another sense is still there. I was rather surprised that no one stopped me then. I assumed it was because there are so many other indications in the air that we have in fact got to revise both concepts pretty soon. I don't know what else to say. *Is* it such an inconceivable idea? Does not theology, for instance, manage to conceive somehow of the Word proceeding from the Father, and yet remaining in the Father?

BURGEON: *Verbum supernum prodiens*
　　　　Nec Patris linquens dexteram....

HUNTER: That is a mystery, and you had better leave it alone.

BURROWS: I don't quite see why he should leave it alone.

HUNTER: I shouldn't expect you to. I *do*.

It was the first time anyone had been actually rude. I should have been even more surprised than I was, if the whole room had not by then become so warm and moist and still that one had the feeling that almost anything might happen, though the most likely thing was thunder.

I myself no longer appeared to have any separate existence inside my shirt. As he sat there in his shirt-sleeves, I saw the perspiration beginning to glisten on Hunter's forehead and at the same time felt it gathering on my own. It was getting quite desperate and I wondered for a moment whether to suggest a break. Before I had made up my mind, however, Hunter went on, in smoother language this time, but with the same edge in his voice:

'You come out into the open rather suddenly, Sanderson, at the end of your long and cautious exposition. You keep insisting that conscious thinking is "your act" ——'

SANDERSON: I was quoting you!

HUNTER: I know. You also say that this thinking can be led from inside the brain to outside it. Do you mean to imply that you yourself can exist outside your body?

SANDERSON: I did not say I could. I said it could be done.

HUNTER: Leaving aside the question of how you know that, could there be a much more loathsome idea? When you brought in clairvoyance, I thought at first you meant some kind of mediumism—which I believe need not always involve a state of trance, though it must always involve an unwarrantable—and incidentally very dangerous—violation of personal integrity. But I see that what you are really advocating is much more like Shamanism. You would have us wandering about in space—and in time, too, if I understood you correctly—outside the body, to collect new data. It may be possible—the anthropologists certainly bring back some queer stories—but if it is, any secrets you might unlock that way are, in my opinion, forbidden secrets; and I'll have none of them.

At this point—to my great relief, since it renewed the opportunity I had just let slip—the thunder broke, and we listened to it rolling round the sky with that menacing relish that seems to proclaim it has been repressed too long in custody and intends to make the most of its discharge and go on doing so for as long as possible.

'The gong!' I said at last. 'Coffee!'

By the time we had finished drinking it a torrent of rain had fallen and a cool breeze had cleared the sultry air. We shut all the windows except one and Hunter and Upwater both resumed their coats, as I crossed the room to switch on the recorder for the last time.

'I don't quite know,' I said as I returned to my seat, 'whether Hunter's last contribution calls for a reply, or whether the question he put should be regarded more as a rhetorical one. But while I have been sipping, and listening to the gentle rain from heaven——'

BRODIE: You'd call it gentle, would you?

BURGEON: Well, no. It was violent while it lasted. But the effects of its violence seem somehow gentle. Anyway, while we have been having our coffee, one reflection has occurred to me, arising out of some of the other things we have been saying here, and perhaps I might begin by trying to formulate it. First of all, I think Hunter has voiced an objection—or is it a distaste? or both?—which a good many people feel and feel very

strongly, to the kind of thing Sanderson appeared to
be advocating. I certainly feel it myself. At one
point, while he was speaking, there came into my
mind that poem of de la Mare's that begins: 'Be not
too wildly amorous of the far' and later—how does
it go?

> Friendly thy body: guard its solitude,
> Sure shelter is thy heart. It once had rest
> Where founts miraculous thy lips endewed,
> Yet nought loomed further than thy mother's breast.

I find the conviction that my spiritual integrity, so far
as I can lay claim to such a lofty possession, is bound
up with my definite location in ... or, if you prefer,
identity with ... my own body—and that any other
view is somehow *unhealthy*—I find this conviction
goes very deep. What I have been wondering in the
last few minutes is, whether I am not rather hoist
with my own petard, having regard to our (*need* we
use the word 'exhibition'?), our old dialogue? I
pressed it all rather hard, you will remember, and it
does seem to follow, if I was right then, that this
deep conviction is after all based on an illusion. It is
rather serious, because, as I say, it is not just an
intellectual conviction, but goes somehow to the roots
of my being—down into the depths, out of which I
seek to choose the healthy and avoid the unhealthy.
That's all I have to say. It seemed only fair to Hunter
to lay this card on the table.

BURROWS: Why do you say it is based on an illusion?

BURGEON: Because, if I was right yesterday, the whole
conception of my mind sitting safely in my body and
looking out through its senses on to a universe which
is *not-mind*, and with which my own mind has
therefore no connection except through the senses, is
an impossible one. The whole picture is an illusion,
and I myself called the whole apparatus, on which
this much-prized 'solitude' is based — a spectre.

SANDERSON: Not everyone is as frank with himself as
you are. I suggest the moral is, that it is one thing to
convince yourself of something intellectually, and
quite another really to *accept* it. In fact, wasn't it
because of this very difficulty that you staged the
dialogue? As far as I am concerned, I found the central
argument of it, as I have said, unanswerable. But I was
not with you when you drove Brodie into admitting
that people are idiots, because they adopt, and even
themselves advance, arguments which disprove the
mindless universe, and yet go on acting, and go on
thinking in their own particular sphere, on the opposite
assumption.

BURGEON: Well, of course, it was part of the Socratic
business to put it at the same time in the politest and
the rudest possible way. I don't know that I'd ——

SANDERSON: I fancy it goes a bit deeper than that. It
might be otherwise if a normal human being were
indeed simply a brain on legs; but he is not. If you
look at the whole of him, in his contrasting but
interpenetrating threefold nature, he is a sort of
delicate funnel, whereby the whole past history of

the world is poured into the present moment. Burrows got into hot water for saying that *what* a man thinks is less important than *why* he thinks it. But, when you find a man's thoughts absurd and inconsistent on one point, though they are otherwise competent enough, isn't Burrows right? And if so, isn't he even more right when you find that happening to large numbers of people through several generations? To the thinking of the modern Western world as a whole?

If we are to choose the simpler hypothesis, surely we must suppose that the Western mind, since the time of Galileo, is not logically idiotic, but that out of its unconscious drives, it has *chosen* to see the universe about it as mindless and to refuse, in the face of all the evidence, to see it in any other way. Isn't it possible that we chose to do so, because it is to that very choice that we owe this valued 'solitude', on which our spiritual integrity and our freedom seem to depend?

BURGEON: That is a very interesting idea. But there is, to say the least, another way of looking at it. It is all very well for you, and Walter de la Mare, and Hunter— yes, and I suppose for me—to prize the 'solitude' as a precious possession. But not everyone feels it that way. There is such a thing as claustrophobia. There is a growing body of literature, and of art, which strongly suggests that it is much more like a curse! Or rather that it is *the* curse, *the* experience which menaces, more and more with every decade that passes, our civilization and even our sanity. The line from Nietzsche to Kafka—Existentialism—the aberrations of contemporary painting—and outside of art and literature, Burrows and his colleagues know something of its evil side. Erich Heller, practically equates it with hell. Read his *Disinherited Mind*, if you haven't done so already. For him—and he is not alone—what he calls 'the loss of significant external reality' was not a blessing—and is proving a catastrophe.

SANDERSON: Surely, it is proving a catastrophe, just because of the empty and distorted idea we now have of our own history!

BURGEON: I don't follow.

SANDERSON: Look into Charles Davy's *Towards a Third Culture* if you want to see how much we have lost on nearly every front by this cutting of our lines of communication, this loss of all real understanding of the traditional wisdom on which our ancestors could still feed; and how much we have gained.

I think the rise of Existentialism also brings it out very clearly. The Existentialists are sharply aware of the causal nexus between the absence of significant external reality on the one hand—and the presence of human freedom on the other. They see the one as correlative to the other; and they feel the full weight of the responsibility which this freedom brings. But because they are blind to the roots of human freedom in the whole evolution of human consciousness, they feel crushed by the weight. They claim that man is responsible for all that exists, and yet the creature that bears this responsibihty is for them a hollow void.

It is different for those who do know something of that evolution, and are seised of the threefold nature of man; for they are aware that it is the function of man to discharge this responsibility by grasping his spiritual inheritance in the new freedom of thought which the scientific revolution has brought in its train, and by uniting it, as knowledge, with his unfettered will. And if they seek to recover that inheritance in the realm from which it stemmed, a realm beyond the brain and the senses, they do so not as an escape, but in order to make its substance available to the earth and to human social life, where an authentic and contemporary wisdom is so sadly lacking, so badly needed. They are as totally involved and committed as any Existentiahst—indeed I would say more so. But *their* responsibility for existence, though no less absolute, is less forlorn. To them also the solitude, the disinheritance, the loss of significant external reality, is a catastrophe; but it is so only as being born is a catastrophe.

BURGEON: If Burrows is right about me and my secrets, I suppose I ought to appreciate the comparison! But it's too oriental a view for me.

SANDERSON: I didn't say it was *mainly* a catastrophe, or a final one. I would have thought there were two ways out of it; the Eastern and the Western way. The Oriental way is to become unborn again. The Occidental way is to grow up. It is now that they are coming to despair of finding their own way, that so many Western minds are turning back to the traditional wisdom of the East. When I said that being born was a catastrophe, I meant rather that you cannot be born without experiencing catastrophe. Every child learns that, when he wakes in the night and finds himself alone. It doesn't happen straight away. First of all the baby is full of beans, feeling out for everything in reach, delighted to find itself arrived 'out of everywhere into here', exploring every sense-impression, pleased with the solidity of things, and occasionally disposing of surplus energy by kicking out and screaming aggressively at the top of its voice. I believe that was about the stage mankind as a whole had got to in the nineteenth century, and the cocksure positivism of a Haeckel or a Herbert Spencer was the delighted kicking and screaming. But the child, the new-born Ego, grows older and, sooner or later, it must wake and find itself alone in the dark and learn the price of self-consciousness.

BRODIE: And what is the poor bairn to do then, in your view?

BURGEON: Or in Rudolf Steiner's!

SANDERSON: Well, it may have been taught to say its prayers. But even if it has—and that is not so likely nowadays—it will never *consciously* desire to get out of its predicament by the way it came. It will want the electric light switched on and everything round it to be as familiar and matter-of-fact and solid as possible. It will hug its own body as a friend and the last thing it will seek is any sort of mystery. But let me drop the analogy. As we see it, the whole outlook brought about by the scientific revolution should have been—must be—a phase, only, of the evolution of consciousness. An absolutely indispensable phase, but a passing one. What is *riveting* it on to us and preventing us from superseding it, because it prevents us from even imagining any other kind of consciousness, is precisely this error of projecting it back into the past. The error that Burgeon was tilting at: our distorted image of history. It is rather as if someone, who had never seen himself before, had learnt for the first time to make a mirror; only he had accidentally made it convex. So that he assumed that he and all men before him were like the little waddling reflection he has just succeeded in producing. It is a terrific achievement to have made a mirror at all. But the justifiable pride he takes in it ought not to prevent him from learning to make a truer one. History, at least any kind of universal history, is still very much in its infancy. Later on, I believe it will be very different and we shall get the true picture of evolution instead of the false one. And then the sort of problem we shall be discussing will be, not how can there possibly be such a thing as consciousness outside the body, and do we want it if there can, but rather: how did human consciousness ever come to contract *into* the body?

UPWATER: I have been trying to follow you as sympa-thetically as possible, suspending judgment rather than raising objections. But it seems to me there is one fatal objection to the whole view you are putting forward. Assume for the sake of argument—and of course it is only for the sake of argument—that the genesis of the individual's mental powers is as you said it was, when you were talking about 'geometrizing'. You now tell us that the evolution of consciousness in mankind as a whole was similar, and you support that with the apparent homology between phylogenesis and ontogenesis.

SANDERSON: I don't think I put it quite as deductively as that. But please go on. I certainly did take things in that order.

UPWATER: I see no relation between the two. You are saying (have I understood you correctly?) that consciousness became more and more individualized, more and more ——

SANDERSON: More and more *self*-consciousness.

UPWATER: ——as it drew into the body, so to speak, from some sort of existence outside it. But to maintain that that happened *phylogenetically* makes nonsense. Where is the continuity? The process is interrupted over and over again by death. In the case of the body itself that doesn't matter, because the individual organism will have reproduced itself before it dies. But, according to your own account, that cannot also apply to its self-consciousness. The whole process, from without to within, happens afresh with each child. How then can you speak of a *gradual* evolution of self-consciousness?

SANDERSON: I would have thought that objection applied more to Chardin's way of putting it. He speaks of a gradual evolution of self-consciousness out of a consciousness which was still 'diffuse' and he seeks to maintain this within the general framework of orthodox evolution, the 'spectral' evolution according to which matter came first and evolved to mind. But that, as you say, is not an evolution of self-consciousness at all. It can at most be an evolution of ephemeral vehicles or organisms which gradually became more capable of *sustaining* self-consciousness. To propound an evolution of self-consciousness out of another kind of consciousness presupposes continuity, so that the evolved self could, as it were, look back to the previous stages in which it was less of a self than it is now.

UPWATER: Very likely. But I was not criticising Chardin. I was criticizing you.

SANDERSON: I know. I really only brought in Chardin, because I think your objection is valid and, if one goes no further than I have so far done, unanswerable. I suppose I must make it clear how much further I do go. I am maintaining that there is really a gradual evolution of self-consciousness out of a consciousness that was extended and unindividualized, rather as the light itself is. And this of course is something quite different from an evolution of organisms, *in* which a flicker of so-called self-consciousness appears from nowhere and vanishes again after a few years. And I did use, at all events for the purposes of illustration, the argument from ontogenesis, to phylogenesis. If the two are really homologous, however, there is something else which follows, and it is this.

If you accept *any* phylogenetic evolution, you must presuppose that the particular form you are studying, from the moment when it emerges *as* a particular form, has had a continuous existence of some sort, an abiding unity through all its variations. True, the form appears only in successive embodiments, which are born and die again. It is an interrupted continuity. But, unless it continues to be *the same* species, whose evolution you are tracing, there is nothing to trace, nothing to study, nothing to talk about.

BURGEON: No subject for the verb 'evolve'!

SANDERSON: In the same way, if you really conceive of a gradual evolution of self-consciousness from some earlier stage of group- or collective- or diffused- or 'sub'-consciousness, it must be the *same* self that continues from the moment it becomes recognizably individual—just as in the other case it had to be the same form. Not the same *sort* of self in different bodies. There is no species called 'self'.

BURGEON: Because each one is 'special'! I rather like this.

SANDERSON: If you like, but don't let us get too linguistic. As Burrows pointed out, when you dig down to the unconscious, or sub-conscious, level, each human being differs essentially from every other. If, then, some evolving 'self' reappears, like a species, in successive embodiments, it must still be the same self. It follows that we must stop talking about an evolution of self-consciousness, unless either we really mean something else, *or* we are prepared to presuppose repeated earth-lives.

UPWATER: Repeated earth-lives! Do you mean reincarnation?

SANDERSON: Yes. I do.

BURGEON: Hm!—too oriental for me.

SANDERSON: It strikes you as oriental, because in modern times we have mostly so far heard about it from the East. That, as I see it, is because the East has never forgotten, as we have, the old cloudy and inaccurate, but *elementally* sound, wisdom which was once universal. The West has chosen to forget or disbelieve it—perhaps as wilfully and unreasonably as you yourself have pointed out it has chosen to believe in a mindless universe.

BRODIE: Why not say 'as idiotically'?

SANDERSON: No, I would say out of the same unconscious drive. Anyway, don't mix up two things. The mere fact of re-birth is no more oriental than the fact of birth. They are both of them neither oriental nor occidental. What you are reacting to is the oriental *attitude* to re-birth—which is in accord with its attitude to birth in general, and consists in regarding it as more of a catastrophe than a blessing, and in the devising of means of escape from it.

BURROWS: Well, we could cure them of that.

BRODIE: You had better get a little further with curing the West first. *So* far, it seems you have only succeeded in getting us into a worse muddle than ever.

DUNN: I fear somebody else has been mixing up two things. Burgeon thinks he has *proved* analytically that the universe is not mindless. Of course he is wrong——

BURGEON: How?

DUNN: Never mind how. There is no longer time for it. The point is, that this gives you at least ostensible grounds for calling us unreasonable. But Sanderson has no such grounds, because he hasn't appealed to reason. He says he bases his remarkable familiarity with the imperceptible on experience. By the way, I suppose that applies to what you have just been saying about reincarnation as much as to anything else?

SANDERSON: Yes. But I hope I haven't been talking unreasonably. If a fact beyond our experience is true, reasonable consideration of related facts within our experience will tend to confirm it. All I maintain is that the experience must come first—somewhere—from someone, who chooses to report it. If what he reports is inherently unreasonable, we shall reject it as untrue. If it is reasonable, we may think it wiser to assume the contrary—at least until we are able to test it for ourselves. That seems to me quite different from the principle of *inferring* from experience to a realm beyond experience. It was this last practice that the scientific revolution got rid of—or should have done.

BRODIE: Then you don't personally remember your previous incarnation?

SANDERSON: Good Lord, no. My unconscious is about as unconscious as the next man's.

BURGEON: And I suppose in this case the 'someone' who reports to us about reincarnation is—Rudolf Steiner?

SANDERSON: Certainly.

BURROWS: We are to accept it because he says he knows it from experience?

BRODIE: No. He didn't say that. You haven't been listening. I suppose, Sanderson, this comes in the second of the two categories you distinguished so carefully, when Burgeon first threw Steiner at your head yesterday? How about the ontogenetic theories (or would you rather I called them 'descriptions'?) you were giving us yesterday—are they the same?

SANDERSON: N-no. Not quite. To a very small degree, I would place them in the first category.

BRODIE: Meaning that you have personally tested or experienced the formative ether, or space, you were speaking of?

SANDERSON: You are driving me rather hard—but, to a very slight degree, yes.

BRODIE: Then you will be able to help us further. I don't mean it ironically. (I say that, because it is just the sort of provoking thing Burgeon kept on saying yesterday, when he was playing Socrates.) When you spoke just now of accepting someone else's report, until we have tested it for ourselves, I recalled some mysterious allusions yesterday to 'strengthened thinking', 'systematic training' and the like. It seems to me it is about time we heard *how* we are supposed to put ourselves in a way to test these reported experiences for ourselves.

Sanderson looked round at us with some diffidence. 'Do you *really* all want me to go on?' he asked. Upwater looked at his watch. 'Better not try and start a new hare at this stage,' he said. 'Please do.'

SANDERSON: Then I suppose I had better begin by referring back to the human trinity, the threefold nature of man, as we see it—thinking at one pole and willing at the other—and the resulting tension between them. If that is all right, the problem of making the unconscious conscious, or at all events *more* conscious, can be seen as the problem of getting our will into our thinking activity. We have somehow to acquire, or re-acquire, the faculty of thinking and observing not merely with the brain and the senses, but with the whole threefold organism. You remember I claimed that this polarity, and the resulting threefold nature, is also implanted in our *physical* organism. So far from denying our psycho-somatic unity, therefore, we have deliberately to make use of it. But to do that we must first achieve it. That is something quite different from leaving it to achieve itself in us. For then *it* makes use of *us*. Then it degenerates to mere instinct.

BURGEON: You would distinguish psycho-somatic unity from somato-psychic unity?

SANDERSON: The one is instinct. The other is spirit. But we do not achieve this unity by forming new *ideas* about the nature of the unconscious, or even about what is going on in our own unconscious, because all that still remains in the one sphere of thinking. I mean something quite different. To some extent we most of us do it already—when we force ourselves to attend closely to something we are not interested in. But it is possible to raise this faculty of attention to a higher power by systematically exercising it—rather as we strengthen a muscle by repeated exercises. To some extent we do strengthen the muscle by ordinary use. But we need special exercises if we decide to develop it to an enhanced and special strength. You do that with willed thinking, if you practise attention to other objects than a *train* of ideas; if you practise regularly, over a long period, concentrating the mind on one single concept or one single object, to the exclusion of all else. Of course it must be a concept without emotional overtones.

That is one thing; and of course it is only the very beginning. I don't see how I can hope to do more than give some sort of crude and fragmentary idea of the *sort* of thing I mean, in case it's really quite unfamiliar to you. To take another example—I stressed the fact that the tension between the two poles of the human being is the basis of his emotional experience, his whole flickering life of feeling. The pursuit of the kind of knowledge, the knowledge in extended experience, which I have argued for, also requires a systematic cultivation of feelings—feelings evoked by selected images and symbols, for instance, and feelings about the processes of nature and her appearances. One must take pains to become able somehow not merely to feel but deliberately to *use* one's feelings as a means to perception; to treat *them* as a precision instrument for investigating quality, just as we take enormous pains to develop external precision instruments for investigating quantity.

BURGEON: There is something awfully unnatural in the idea of deliberately setting out to feel—as a means to an end.

UPWATER: And what possible guarantee have you got, when you have done, that what you suppose is objective 'experience' is not simply your own deliberately induced feelings hypostatized?

SANDERSON: Remember I am assuming that your powers of attention and thought-control have previously been strengthened. In other words that you are exceptionally wide-awake. To full waking consciousness immediate experience is its own guarantee. You can't go behind it. I agree with Dunn there, but I don't agree with his limitation of experience to what he calls 'normal'. We have really been through all that. Somebody— Burrows—drew attention to this trick of picking out the simplest examples and leaving out all the rest. Does, for instance, the 'normal' include any element of active imagination? And if so, why must it be just so much and no more? Burgeon knows very well that, when we experience a symbol, its symbol-nature is part of the experience itself, not something we infer abstractly after first experiencing it as literal.

BURGEON: Everyone who has learnt to *read* knows it! He has learnt to experience as symbols what he formerly experienced only as squiggles!

SANDERSON: Well, yes; and which of the two experiences is 'normal'? But I gather no one wants to go back over all that. I will finish as quickly as I can. Perhaps I ought to try to give some detailed example, however hurriedly selected, and to show how it applies to the rest of what I have been saying.

BRODIE: You certainly ought.

SANDERSON: One of our commonest experiences of the face of nature is what I might call the spring and autumn experience. The different forms and colours and smells that we perceive on the one hand in growing and on the other hand in decaying things. To some extent we already 'read' them rather than merely perceive them, for the inner processes of growth and decay which they express are qualitatively part of our perception—unless we are idiots. Now we *may* choose, instead of casually noticing all this and perhaps poetizing it, really to concentrate on the qualities and on the processes they betoken, and then deliberately to cultivate strong feelings about them. I don't of course mean emotions of melancholy or hopefulness, but something much more impersonal— more akin, perhaps, to our experience of the minor and major keys in music. Again, we can experience, both in observation and feeling, the alternate expansion and contraction, which characterizes the growth-process itself—most noticeably in plants—to which

Goethe drew attention with such delicacy in his book on *The Metamorphosis of Plants*. (I confess that condensing it in this shorthand way gives me a feeling of nakedness—still, one *can* do so.) Of course it is only a first feeble step, but eventually, as a result of that and of many other steps in the same direction, one may come to a direct experience of those formative, structure-bestowing forces from space, of which I tried to speak before. One becomes, to use a metaphor, really acquainted with Huxley's 'invisible artist' and able to study his modelling movements in detail. And you can use these detailed observations, as is already being done, for quite practical purposes— therapeutic, agricultural and so on.

BRODIE: I followed you sympathetically in the first part of what you said—when you were talking about strengthening the thinking-power; but when you go on to bring in feeling—that is another matter altogether.

SANDERSON: And yet it is surely obvious that we cannot closely approach familiar nature in any other way. There is no other road to a science of the qualitative. Take colour, for instance. You can treat it spectrally (in both senses of the word!) as waves or vibrations. But in doing so you lose colour itself altogether. For we never actually experience the vibrations. If you want to investigate colour as a quality, you are obliged to approach it—as Goethe did—without forgetting our normal experience of it as a sort of bridge between the outer world of perception and the inner world of feeling. That is why the people who are

practically concerned with the *quality* of colour—
because their bread and butter comes from colour-
printing or colour-reproduction—are at present busy
studying Goethe's theory of colour, or rediscovering
it for themselves.

BRODIE: Yes. But the idea of systematically making *use*
of our feelings—calling up this feeling or that, and
dismissing it when we have no further use for it!
What becomes of the thing called 'sincerity'?

BURGEON: There is perhaps this to be said. Sincerity seems
to have become a rather ticklish problem anyhow.
Are not people getting more and more aware, often
against their will, of a something in themselves that
is not quite identified with their feelings, even the
strongest or even the deepest ones? Isn't that just the
malaise which has been creeping over the whole
world of literature since the decline of Romanticism?
It seems to lead either to a strained emphasis on
physical violence *à la* Hemingway, or more often to
that kind of motiveless and unpointed irony that you
find simply *everywhere* nowadays; but especially in
poetry, which still cannot quite help having to do with
feeling. We dare not *surrender* to any feeling, however
serious, for more than a few seconds at a time. As
soon as we have expressed it, we feel an impulse to
deny our own identity with it, to withdraw from it
and add sardonically, or drily, with T. S. Eliot: 'That
was a way of putting it.'

SANDERSON: I could hardly agree more. Would you say
the *malaise* shows any signs of wearing off?

BURROWS: I doubt it. Conflicts between separate parts of the mind, functioning more or less independently, grow increasingly common. Indeed it is one of the principal situations with which a practising psychiatrist has to deal.

BURGEON: I doubt it too. As far as literature is concerned, there are half-hearted revolts against it from time to time, but by and large I would say it is steadily getting worse. I suppose that is one reason why Eliot still goes down so well even with the young; and why people just can't stop writing books about him. After all he was the first to express it in English, unless you count Pearsall Smith, and I don't know that anyone has done it better since.

SANDERSON: I suggest that the *malaise* comes of our timid refusal to accept this detachment as something that is in fact happening in the world. Self-consciousness, no longer nascent, but actually born, is unobtrusively forcing us, as it comes into its own, to overhaul even our concept of sincerity.

Upwater, in terms of biological evolution, has not an over-development of complexity sometimes preceded the appearance of a new phylum?

UPWATER: Yes. The complexity is suddenly abandoned in favour of a new simplicity at a higher level—or it may be internalized, as when sensation based on brain and nerves arose to replace the elaborate mechanism by which insects connect up with their environment.

SANDERSON: It is conceivable that the same sort of new development may be in store for self-consciousness.

BURGEON: Certainly there is something rather insect-like about introspective bombination. I am thinking of people like Henry James and Virginia Woolf. A self-consciousness which is at once too subtle and too cumbrous—too cumbrous, because too *obviously* subtle. Fussy and restless—compelled to be so by the limited reach of its feelers.

SANDERSON: If only we would go on to a new concept of sincerity, instead of trying to creep back to the outmoded one, which will no longer have us in its lap, we might in the end reach a rather different relation to our own feelings. Instead of having an uneasy sense of insincerity because we remain aware of something in us which exists apart from, or alongside of, or outside of them, we should dwell in the midst of them, guiding perhaps and enlightening them, but no more needing to disclaim them than the sun needs to disclaim the planets.

BURGEON: Let us get back to the main thread. We have been digressing from what was itself a digression. Perhaps it was necessary; but if I remember rightly, the minutes would read something like this: Sanderson said yesterday (after some talk about phylogenesis and ontogenesis) that his theory of evolution was not simply a theory, but was a matter of actual observation. Someone—Hunter, I think—pointed out that we cannot anyway observe the past. Sanderson (I remember this quite clearly) disagreed. But at that point he was led off into an argument about the theory of perception. Then, somehow or other, there was a sort of excursus on the evolution of self-consciousness—which he said implied reincarnation. We looked like getting back then to Hunter's original objection, but Brodie took him off into an account of how the process of thinking and perceiving can be strengthened or developed; and now we are getting away even from that. It is not Sanderson's fault, but it seems to me he has not yet attempted to meet the objection it all began with. All he has done is to put up a sort of *argumentum ad hominem* to Dunn, claiming that in Dunn's view of the nature of science (which in some mysterious way he himself seems nevertheless to accept) you could never have a science dealing with the past at all. Is that right?

BRODIE: I think so. Yes.

BURGEON: Then what about the objection, Sanderson?

SANDERSON: Our time's getting very short, but I'll do my best. You must remember the position I start from: that the material world is condensed from a spiritual origin and that the individual self has evolved from that same origin. Now those who believe the opposite get at any knowledge they have of the remote past—how shall I put it—*vestigially*. They try to observe the past in its present outcome by examining the geological and fossil 'record of the rocks' and so forth. We both agree that the present substance, form and condition of anything is the outcome of its past development, but it must make all the difference of course whether that past is wholly material or whether it is also immaterial. If what I was saying earlier is right, it follows, I think, that the objects of the natural world will be vestiges of their primeval spiritual origin as well as of their subsequent physical development. This will apply to all objects phylogenetically speaking and, in the case of living organisms, it will also apply ontogenetically. For both of us nature is, in a manner of speaking, history displayed; only the histories are very different. For more recent periods I suppose both views may be to some extent right; but go far enough back and one of the two must be wrong.

Secondly I have maintained that the immaterial realm from which the material is derived is accessible to direct observation by a human being who has trained himself adequately to the task.

Now I have still to try and meet the objection that this does not explain how anyone could actually observe the past. And I think here I can only refer back to what I said yesterday—that the whole relation of past and present, the whole nature of time, is different in the spiritual, or if you like, in the unconscious realm. I suppose that sounds rather bald. But really *everything* changes its aspect as soon as you start from somewhere else. Most people feel that their mental experience is a kind of replica of nature; but *we* feel nature herself as a replica of mind. Burgeon at least seemed to agree with this in theory, when he was talking about symbolism and the origin of language.

Need we go again into the relation between 'thinking' and 'I think'? To say that nature is history displayed is really to say that nature is man's unconscious being, displayed objectively before him. I don't think it matters much whether you put it that way or whether you say, with Goethe—and to some extent with Chardin and perhaps even Upwater— that human consciousness is the mirror in which nature surveys herself. The point is, that in the unconscious, whether you call it man's or nature's, the whole relation between past and present, the whole nature of time, has to be conceived differently. We get a hint of it in dreams. The past remains latent in the present, perhaps in something the same way as it does in the meaning of a word. I don't think I can be more precise. I could not be without beginning to speak of hierarchies of creative beings, and there is obviously no time for that, even if you wanted it.

When I speak of experiencing, or observing, the past, rather than theorizing about it, I mean roughly that it is possible with trained powers to reconstitute nature as history—to reconvert it, as it were, from history displayed into history remembered. Remembered in the detailed manner of its display. Of course it is memory in a somewhat different sense from ordinary memory; but even ordinary memory is nearer to observation than it is to theory or inference.

BURGEON: I am interested to know whether all this applies only to what you called the 'primeval' period, or whether these 'trained powers' have direct access also to the prehistoric period—perhaps even to the historic.

SANDERSON: They are not necessarily limited to the remote past. And I have already said that emergence from the immaterial into the material is ontogenetic as well as phylogenetic.

BURGEON: I was thinking more particularly of the present furious interest in archaeology. From what little I know of it, if ever there was an example of a precariously inverted pyramid of theory on a very slender apex of fact, there you have it. When I compare the sort of theories that are put forward about the consciousness of primitive man with the indications you get by pursuing a more internal route—myth and the study of language, I confess it has sometimes seemed to me that there *must* be a more satisfactory way of getting back into our own past than all this measuring of potsherds and arrowheads.

SANDERSON: Believe me, there is. It is not a question of having to jump suddenly back to the *remote* past. I have already said that the human physical organism reproduces as it were all three periods; it is the lower organs that embody our most unconscious part and it is these you will study if you want to experience the remoter past. But you may also study, for instance, the brain and nerves.

Perhaps I shouldn't have used the word 'study'; though you would certainly have to study them in the ordinary physiological sense as well. But it is more a question of rendering conscious the unconscious element in you, of which your different organs are functions. Brain, heart, liver, spleen have been built into your body by the world, by the whole history of the world, and if you 'study' one of them in that intensive way, you have access to the relevant period of world-history. Access, first of all, to the building that was going on before your birth and, through that, back into their remoter phylogenesis.

You see—or at any rate I have argued—that if evolution has indeed been fundamentally the evolution of self-consciousness, there cannot be that sharp break between ontogenetic and phylogenetic development, which the positivist picture of evolution assumes. The one must merge gradually back into the other.

BRODIE: I am beginning to feel as Burgeon said he did yesterday—only *he* didn't mean it—giddy! I don't really understand how we keep swinging from space to time and back again. You started on us yesterday with a kind of disquisition on the nature of space. Then there was more about evolution. Then this morning the talk was all of getting outside the body; so much so that you were accused of propounding Shamanism. And now here we have been for the last ten minutes or more grinding away at the business of getting back somehow in time—as if space were no longer of any importance.

SANDERSON: I'm sorry, Brodie. I haven't marshalled my material at all well and you must think me scatterbrained.

BRODIE: I certainly don't think that; but I *am* giddy.

SANDERSON: I suppose there hasn't been much order or system in our whole symposium. But we do seem in

a way to have come full circle. It began with you and
Ranger talking at length about space, and then
Upwater chipped in with the objection that you had
left out time. Then we got on to the unconscious
mind. Burgeon maintained that the unconscious mind
must really be conceived of as present in nature.
Well—nature and space—you can hardly have one
without the other. I suppose I came in with the
suggestion that, in the unconscious mind, we have
access to a sort of *pre*-nature, the cosmic space out of
which nature comes into being. And I said we could
not get into it consciously without a kind of turning
inside out. Probably it's high time I left off!

BRODIE: There are a good many loose ends left untied.

SANDERSON: I'm afraid that's inevitable ... all right ...
look ... at the end of a hand of bridge people
sometimes just throw the last three or four cards on
the table, anyhow, in any sort of order. I'll try doing
the same. Whether it's because I've won or lost the
game, I'll leave to you.

Or perhaps it's the other way round. I've only
played the first three or four cards and it is all the
rest that are to go on the table! Never mind. Here
goes:

Man is a threefold being, threefold through and
through, both in his body and his soul. His conscious
mind is at one pole and his unconscious at the other.
Consciousness and unconsciousness are mutually
exclusive; but the mutual exclusion of two opposite
poles is resolved in the tension between them and

the motion it begets. In the case of the spiritual polarity between conscious and unconscious the motion begotten is rhythmic—it finds expression in the course of time and the various rhythms of nature. Consciousness and unconsciousness are by definition alternative states. How then can the one evolve gradually into the other? The antagonism between alternatives can to begin with be mitigated by a wise *alternation*, (Perhaps, after all, Box and Cox's landlady turns out to be the Wise Woman!) The characteristic rhythmic alternation is between consciousness and unconsciousness: sleeping and waking. The soul is not created afresh every morning; but this, its major oscillation between its unconscious extreme and its conscious, is normally in phase with the terrestrial rhythm of darkness and light, or night and day.

I believe I have already suggested that *colour* is the most obvious bridge between emotion and perception, that is, between subjective experience of the psyche and quality objective in nature. Both light up only *between* the extremes of light and darkness, and in their reciprocal interplay. Thus, outwardly the rainbow— or, if you prefer it, the spectrum—is the bridge between dark and light, but inwardly the rainbow is, what the soul itself is, the bridge between body and spirit, between earth and heaven.

But there are also shorter and less sharp alternations between a *more* conscious and a less conscious state. If you examine them, inbreathing and outbreathing, and the systole and diastole of the heart will be found to be of this nature. And there are also larger rhythms, such as the seasons. We are thrust in more on ourselves, wakened up, in the winter. We dream ourselves out into space in the summer. And above all there is the rhythm of birth and death; alternate existence here on earth and, for much longer intervening periods, in the spiritual world. By 'spiritual world' I mean an immaterial realm beyond space and containing it, from which the physical world is brought into being. It is a realm in which we participate with our own activity, so far as that activity is mental. Each time we die, we must expand through space and beyond it into that realm, where with our mind we nevertheless remain domiciled even during our life on earth. We take back from each embodiment on earth, or we may do so, an increasing power of retaining our self-consciousness during this other phase. We bring back from there to earth, or we may do so, an increasing recollection of the strength and grace which our sojourn in the spheres has bestowed on us. That, as we see it, is the process of human and cosmic evolution.

If it bears at all the stamp of truth, it is the less surprising that Burgeon here and others should find in a persistent image of paradise the symbol of symbols, or that they should detect that image not only in actual myth and symbol, but also in the face of nature herself—when it is seen as a face and not simply stared at as a spectral mask with nothing, or what have you, behind it. Or that Burrows, and those whom he follows, should trace that image above all in the particular bit of nature with which the subconscious mind simply cannot help remaining on more intimate terms; I mean the human body, its form and its functional drives—half lovely, half distorted relic of the weightless paradisal harmony from which it has shrivelled and shrunk to what it is. Or again that, in spite or in defiance of the persistent undertow—and yet also, in a way, because of it—nearly all of us are impelled to seek comfort in the very walls of our prison cells; that, whether from fear of the unknown or even from an intensity of devotion, or maybe from an obscure blend of the two, we should seek to rely for spiritual support and security on our very confinement away from those blessings.

For then it would be not only through its Adamic origin in the bosom of the race that the longing of the psyche harks back to its source. It would have returned there from time to time to refresh itself at the miraculous founts; and would have experienced other and lesser falls. It would be concealing in itself the recollection of a much more recent involvement in that harmony, namely during the time before its last conception; and, between conception and birth, of a state intermediate between that and this, while the body into which it was once more slowly waning still floated in the waters of life—in the 'glairy fluid' where the invisible artist works. The head first, as the rounded image of the global sphere—the 'mundane shell', as Blake called it—through which it must travel, or rather (since the word is misleading and only a rocket or a Shaman *travels* in space) through which it must contract, on its inward path from the realm beyond space. And, within the skull's protecting shell, the brain that is to bind it all points ... [he paused and looked at Dunn] ... to bind it indivisibly to the sensations of this one body. And then, almost as an afterthought or appendage, the pliant and mobile limbs and their existential organs of nutrition and reproduction, prompt to energize, without compelling, its ultimate return in hard-won independence to the cosmic harmony from which it sprang. And, between the two extremes, the heart and lungs, which will not cease during the term of his exile from their endeavour to keep the peace between the driving energy of the man's will and the receptive tranquillity of his perception and thought. That, or something like it, is the relation between man and nature as we see it.

BURGEON: It is impressive. But is it really any more than yet another 'model'? There have been so many of them; and they seem to depend so much on what happens to be preoccupying our minds at the moment. There was Paley's watch, while mechanism was all the rage. And then, with the rise of industrialism and the danger of overpopulation, Malthus's theory drew everyone's attention, and a struggle for existence was substituted as the result. As a result of that result everyone got interested in biology and we began to interpret everything in terms of organic growth. We rather left out decay, until Spengler came in and the model of organic growth and decay was applied to the rise and decline of civilizations—and to most other things. That seems to be about where we are now. You yourself tell us that Goethe saw the process of organic growth—or was it growth and decay?—in terms of expansion and contraction. You say that you develop your powers of cognition by meditating intensively on growth and decay. Is it surprising that the resulting model of the universe is mainly one of alternating expansion and contraction?

SANDERSON: You have fastened rather too much on one particular meditation, which I really mentioned only as an example. However, I don't deny that it is an important one. The real point is, that there is a difference between what I tried so lamely to describe and merely preoccupying oneself with an *idea* and then transferring it elsewhere as a thought-model. I did go into it at some length, and no one will want me to do it all over again. We actually have the forces of growth and decay in ourselves. Strengthening the *act* of thinking can result in our positively experiencing these forces, and ultimately in our experiencing their provenance. That is really quite different from thinking *about* them.

BRODIE: But you also say that you do not experience them yourself, or only in a very elementary way? Would it be right to say that nearly all you have just told us comes under category two of what you owe to Rudolf Steiner, rather than category one?

SANDERSON: Yes. I would agree with that.

BURGEON: So that your claim that the substance of your description is a matter of experience and not of theory, is not itself based on your own experience?

SANDERSON: I am not an advanced spiritual scientist, I am only a humble student. But then neither am I an advanced physical scientist. And there are a lot of things I accept on the faith that, *if* I were properly trained, and *if* I had the higher mathematical ability which I am not even capable of acquiring with the brain-structure at my disposal in my present life, I could verify them for myself. How does one arrive at these convictions? The more you find they accord with what you have experienced and what you do know—the more you find, though not quite in Ranger's limited sense, that they 'work'—the more seriously you find yourself taking them. Incidentally they *have* been found to work even in Ranger's sense of the word, in a good many applications.

BURROWS: Yes. But there is not only *one* advanced physical scientist. I make it my business to acquaint myself to some extent with what is being said and written by queers of all sorts, especially if they have a substantial following, and I did once have a look at the Steiner movement. Their weak spot is that in practice it is all Steiner himself and what he said. They tell you that the clairvoyant faculties he acquired can be acquired by anyone, but on their own showing the movement has been in existence for fifty years or more without producing anyone in

the same street with him—or even in the next street
but one. Descriptions like the one you have just given
us are all traceable to Steiner, never to his followers.
It is not just Steiner first and the rest nowhere; it is
Steiner in the field and the rest non-starters.

SANDERSON: I think, if you went a little more into detail,
you would find that his followers *have* added a little
here and there. But by and large the complaint is
justified; and in that respect, though not at the point
on which I actually brought it to bear, the analogy
with ordinary science falls to the ground. It is a pity
that it should be so; but when you appreciate more
fully the factors on which spiritual science depends, it
is much less surprising to find one particular individual
so far ahead of the race. Ability in spiritual science does
not depend only on mental training in the ordinary
sense nor only on mental training in the special sense
which I have tried to define. In the last resort it
depends on a principle that is alien to our present
ideas though it has been, and is, acknowledged at
almost all times and places except in the West during
the last few hundred years. I mean the principle of
initiation. Anyone who knows anything about it at
all knows that according to that principle a person
does not become an initiate merely by growing more
acute or more learned; he has actually to become a
different kind of man. Even the degenerate caricatures,
which are what we mostly hear about, all bear
witness to this *principle*. And no one who has dug a
little way beneath the caricatures to find out what is

really at stake, will have much difficulty in concluding that one really great initiate in, say, a thousand years, would be a generous ration.

UPWATER: You are certainly keeping us well supplied with novelties. Before we have finished our attempts at digesting one titbit, you pop yet another into our gaping mouths!

SANDERSON: Titbits? I suppose I was drawn into talking too glibly about getting outside the body.

DUNN: How long, O Lord! How long?

SANDERSON: If so, it was because I have come to see more clearly during this week-end that even the ordinary man is being inexorably impelled towards becoming an extraordinary man. A man able, for instance, not only to *be* his own emotion; but to guide and direct and use it in the service of evolution. This, I begin to see, is the end-product, to which that self-conscious detachment of ourselves from ourselves that we have just spoken of is the early, awkward, hobbledehoy approach. It is either to this, or to despair that we will be driven by our hapless predicament between two terrors—the terror of our positivist solitude in the body and the terror of transcending it. We have seen the kind of double-think the human intelligence will resort to rather than admit to itself the bare possibility of being outside the body. But there are other indications; indeed, I would think that the current hysteria over space-travel had something to do with it. There *is* this instinct to get away outside into space; and there *is* this fear of it. If only we could get outside the body and yet take the body with us!

But I imagine it will be a long time before these pressures are recognized for what they are; and in the meantime, for us ordinary men, the mind is indeed bound *indivisibly* to the brain and the senses; and there are only two ways of disentangling it. One of which is death and the other initiation. The relation or resemblance between the two is also something which transpires through every recorded tradition. It is not only intellectual development, or only intellectual and emotional development, that will serve to accomplish it. Death is not a jest; the threshold between man's conscious and his unconscious is not a jest; the ordeal connoted by initiation is to be sustained only by moral integrity and moral energy raised to a power not ordinarily encountered.

UPWATER: When all that is said, the fact remains that you place this enormous weight on the researches (we will assume they deserve the name) of one man. How can you dare to use the word 'science' in such a context? Its whole essence has been the free co-operation of many minds.

SANDERSON: And I believe in the long run it will continue to be so. But nature—and you regard man as a part of nature—makes unlikely jumps ahead from time to time. Advance raids, as it were, with which the main body takes a long time to catch up. You said a good deal about mutations on Friday evening. But you also suggested that the spearhead of evolution was now to be found in humanity and in the social and mental rather than in the biological sphere; moreover, that it had come to depend more and more on human volition. If I remember right, you also said that it had been gathering itself for a new advance. Are you sure that the new advance, or the new mutation, will be of the kind which you expect or in the form which you had previously imagined? Would it even *be* new if that were the case?

UPWATER: I see well enough what you are driving at. But you have just said that what you call initiation is *not* new—as indeed I know for myself it is not. It is as old as the hills.

SANDERSON: I said the *principle* was not new. But I also remember saying at some earlier stage that I believed the scientific revolution to be *the* great achievement of the human spirit. I do not think we should rule out the possibility that an initiation achieved after that point in the evolution of consciousness may be as different from one achieved before it as initiation itself is different from ordinary consciousness.

Nobody, it seemed, had anything to say to this and after a few moments of unaccustomed silence I turned towards Hunter. 'You haven't opened your mouth since the coffee-break,' I said. 'I wonder why. It's not like you!' 'I have been listening,' he replied. 'And to do you justice,' I said, 'that *is* like you.' 'If I haven't spoken,' Hunter went on, 'it's because I had nothing to say. The trouble is that at bottom I don't think I am very deeply interested. Certainly not in the way you and Sanderson and Upwater—and perhaps Brodie—are. When it comes to the point, I find that, as Wodehouse puts it, "I am not much of a lad for evolution".'

UPWATER: Would you care to expand that at all?

HUNTER: I don't mean I've got a rival theory. The question is rather how much, in the long run, *any* theory really matters. It does matter, of course, in the same way that any legitimate subject of scientific inquiry matters. And in the same way as the general question of scientific method matters. All these things matter, as long as the end proposed is knowledge. But when people begin to attach some kind of religious significance, either to a particular bit of knowledge, or to knowledge in general, another question is automatically raised; a question which would have been left sleeping if they had been content to seek knowledge either for technological purposes or as a value in itself. It is the question of *relative* values. For me, knowledge is valuable, as many other things are valuable, poetry for instance, and painting, or beauty in nature or courtesy or good taste. It is absurd to try and compare them, and erect a scale of values, so that two pounds of good poetry would be equal to one pound of honour, or something like that. It is absurd, *unless* someone attempts to equate any of them with the values of religion. I regard any such attempt as fallacious, because from that point of view it is obvious to me that science or knowledge is a harmless pursuit, and a perfectly legitimate way of spending one's time, but no more.

DUNN: I couldn't agree more.

HUNTER: As to any religious significance it has, I conceive knowledge may be used by God, like most other pursuits, as a means of teaching good men to do His will. When you have said that, you have said all there is to say. The fact remains that the scientific revolution and all the discoveries that followed it are less *important* than a single generous act performed by an ignoramus; and the beautiful pictures of evolution drawn by Upwater or Sanderson are as useful, if we like to make them so, as the illustrations in a child's hornbook.

UPWATER: I am not much of a lad for religion; but I would have thought that any inquiry into the origin and destiny of the human race must have some bearing on it.

HUNTER: Not for those who are satisfied that all we need know about them has already been revealed.

RANGER: I suppose if you believe in revelation, you aren't allowed to believe it goes on, like science does, but you have to believe it just happened once and then stopped!

BURROWS: Whatever beliefs we hold about the value and the ultimate source of their revelations, it was the unconscious, rising to the surface, out of which the prophets spoke. There seems to be no logical or physiological reason why the technique should not be re-acquired. Whether there is any point in calling it 'initiation'....

BURGEON: Even for the satisfied, I should have thought Upwater's inquiry might have a considerable bearing

on our *interpretation* of the revelation. How do we
know we are attaching the right meaning to the words
it was uttered in? All we do know is that they have
nearly all meant very different things at different times.

SANDERSON: Is not such a lofty detachment from history—
in its widest sense, which includes evolution—more
appropriate to the oriental religions? Hindus and
Buddhists can write off history because they regard
time itself as a deplorable illusion. But surely that
also involves writing off the whole Judaeo-Christian
incision into history as part of the illusion?

HUNTER: Why should Christians be specially interested
in the niceties of the relation between nature and the
human mind? How does it bear on either of the two
great commandments?

BRODIE: I fancy we cannot love our neighbour as ourselves
without loving God, and I believe that the more we
know God the more we are likely to love Him.

HUNTER: But what has knowing nature got to do with
knowing God?

DUNN: Amen!

BURGEON: That is the purest positivism. You assume the
spectre, as they all do; the theologians just as much
as the scientists and psychologists. My secret belief is
that it is because they rather *like* it!

SANDERSON: I do not believe that positivism is incompatible
with religion; there are plenty of people who combine
the two; or with the view that history is bunk; but I
do believe that Christianity is incompatible with
either.

HUNTER: Why?

SANDERSON: Because it is based on an historical event that took place in Judaea in the reign of Tiberius, and because that event was an incarnation. What has positivism to do with incarnation? But it is too serious a matter. It would have to be the beginning of a new symposium, not the tail-end of an old one. I can only say what I have said already, that, for us, both birth and evolution *are* incarnation. It would be strange if the phylogenetic embodiment of the macrocosm in the microcosm had nothing to do with the first instant of its ontogenetic achievement. It would be strange if the one were not a symbol of the other; strange if that instant were not the central point of the whole process of evolution; and equally strange if the great paradigm of death and resurrection after three days had nothing to do with initiation.

BURROWS: You would claim, I suppose, that that is why the symbol of the cross so often marks an inner threshold which the dreamer is both impelled and afraid to cross?

SANDERSON: As to knowledge of nature and knowledge of God, if knowledge is the doing of a jig-saw puzzle with atomic events, there is no more to be said. But if it is really a participation through the symbol in the symbolized, it is a different matter. It is a different matter if the sequence of a divergent followed by a convergent evolution is a positive fact and not just a cleverly invented analogy; if humanity was originally one and indistinguishable in the unconscious and is now aiming to become both one and many in full consciousness. Suppose that Burgeon and I are right: then, in the meantime, nature *is* the unconscious, represented. And if that, or something like it, is the case, I submit that our knowledge of nature is very relevant indeed; for it is only by ceasing to regard nature as a spectre that we can hope to inherit her as a kingdom. And it is only in that kingdom that our common destiny can be fulfilled. In the meantime— but we *are* in the meantime, and not we alone. The timeless perspective that can see all round history may be the perspective—may indeed be the only possible perspective—of God the Father, and therefore also of the oriental type of monism which claims an immediate identity with Him. I am content to leave that claim to Dunn's pupil and Burrows's patient. But for me—and I would have thought for any Christian— the other two Persons of the Trinity are of equal status with Him and I would find it arrogant to attempt to place myself beyond them, as I do in placing myself beyond history.

HUNTER: There is also—my gifted friend—a kind of arrogance which disguises itself as humility. You do ill, in my opinion, to drag in the Holy Trinity in defence of your not ignoble humanism.

BURGEON: We are getting back to St. Joan again! What was it? 'A diabolical pride masquerading as a saintly humility!'

HUNTER: That was the Inquisitor's description of Protestantism. Humanism normally leaves out the masquerade. But this seems to be a new sort of humanism.

BURGEON: Why do you keep on dragging in humanism?

HUNTER: Because Sanderson is a humanist. I should have thought that was obvious from his whole vocabulary. His God is man's unconscious.

BURGEON: I don't think the humanists I know would be very pleased to be bracketed with him.

HUNTER: No, because when they use the word, they really mean positivism. I suppose scientific humanism is much the same thing—and most of them have never heard of any other. There is no sport for the ignoramus like killing a useful word. But Sanderson is obviously not an ignoramus and I doubt if he himself would disagree. He might even regard it as a compliment. Do you regard yourself as a humanist, Sanderson?

SANDERSON: People have been known to answer one question by asking another. May I do so now?

HUNTER: It depends on the question.

SANDERSON: Do you believe that you were not only created by God but are sustained at every moment by His Spirit?

HUNTER: Yes... but not in the way you mean.

SANDERSON: Then I am a humanist, but not in the way *you* mean.

HUNTER: Let us not dispute about words.

I looked at my watch. 'I am afraid,' I said, 'the time is rapidly approaching, when we shall have to stop disputing about anything! However it may be with revelations, trains are things that occur once and *don't* stop—or not for very long.'

It was true, and I had been wondering for some time what would be the best way of bringing our symposium to a close. Should I attempt to sum it up myself in a few well-chosen words? It seemed hopeless. An alternative possibility was to ask each in turn for his impression. But that smacked of journalism and in any case there was no longer time for it. Yet I felt there must be some sort of coda, and I had just determined on a third plan.

'Suppose,' I said, 'it should prove possible to repeat this experiment—say in three or four years' time—and it is all too likely that it won't—how would you all feel about it?' 'I should try to come,' said Brodie. 'So should I,' said Ranger. 'I doubt if I'm much use to you—or you to me, perhaps—but it's a good thing to get away from the boys sometimes.'

'Burrows?'

'Yes. I should certainly try. Apart from anything else it's a good exercise for me.'

'You can definitely count me in,' said Sanderson.

'You must count me out, I'm afraid,' said Dunn, who had been yawning a good deal.

'And you, Upwater?'

'Yes.... I *think* so ... anyway ask me and see!' 'And lastly, what about you. Hunter?'

'I hardly think so. You've heard what I have just been saying. But you can always ask me.'

'I think you ought to come,' I said. 'Who knows what may have happened by then? Perhaps Brodie will be telling us that the proton has gone the way of the atom. (I believe it is already *in extremis* and showing marked signs of its approaching dissolution.) And if Upwater still hasn't discovered the missing link, Ranger may have come on it—with the help of Burrows—somewhere in the space-time ambience of the sun's atmosphere. As to Sanderson, I hesitate to surmise what may have happened to *him!*'

'Perhaps,' said Sanderson, 'he will have stopped talking!'

It had begun wth my visit to St. Peter's and it ended with a letter I got from Hunter about a week later. He assured me that, whatever he might have said on the last day, he had found the symposium as a whole, a very interesting and worthwhile experiment and he congratulated me on having undertaken and carried through a truly heroic enterprise. He was really writing to thank me. 'I liked Brodie,' he wrote, 'but'—and there followed a few trenchant comments on some of the other participants. 'By the way,' the letter went on, 'you and I have occasionally swapped dreams, and I had a very odd one two or three nights ago. Here it is.

'There were two tall, solid, heavy doors in front of me, made of some kind of metal—bronze I suppose, something like Ghiberti's doors to the Baptistery in Florence but with even better carvings on them. (This was not surprising, as I knew I had done the carving myself!) I also knew that they hadn't been opened for a very long time. I observed with some alarm that they were now beginning to move, and stood waiting for what would happen next. Some kind of music began to sound, I am not sure whether from within the doors or above or behind me. Then three figures came out of the dark interior one after the other, with short intervals between them, and after looking at or at any rate standing in front of me, for a few moments, they either passed on or disappeared. Not much in that, but now for the three men (if that is the right word)! I can't remember how they were dressed. It was only their heads or "what seemed their heads" that counted. The first had on his shoulders a kind of round box with two holes in it, rather like one of those turnips they say boys used to pierce and put a candle in, to make a bogy. And, by Jove, there must have been a candle in this one, or rather a mort of candles, for light was blazing out of its eye-holes in all directions. It disappeared, and I wondered what was coming next.

'When it did come, it turned out to be a man with a lion's head on him. But an emblematic sort of lion with a very emphatic mane—spread out in rays—you know, the kind that suggests those old woodcuts of the sun. I didn't see if he had a tail and didn't think about it. By the way, I ought to have mentioned, in describing the first apparition, that there were *words* as well. I can't say now whether they were spoken, or I just heard them, or they may even have been written on a sort of inscribed scroll, like the title of a seal or an emblem. Anyway the words the first time were **Subjective Idealism.**

'It was the same with the second figure, only this time the words were **The Key of the Kingdom.** And now came the third.

'If I had been awake, I suppose I should say I was ready for anything by this time—and also that I was surprised all the same by what did emerge. But is one really *surprised* by anything that happens in a dream? Anyway this time, if you please, it was a man with no head at all! I can't recall whether he just hadn't got one, or whether he was carrying it in the normal way under his arm. But this time the "scroll" or title was disappointingly unoriginal. It was simply: **The Kingdom.**

'One more thing. You know how unrelated your feelings often are, in a dream, to what is actually going on. You may await with your hair standing on end some perfectly ordinary event like the sunrise; contrariwise you may see, and even go through, the most horrifying experiences without turning a hair.

'Well, all three figures were grotesque enough and the last was getting on for a Horror Comic. But the *atmosphere* of the dream was exactly the opposite. I don't know whether the music (imagine the Elysian bit in Gluck's *Orpheus* multiplied by about ten) had anything to do with it. It doesn't matter. The point was that, in spite of the touch of alarm, the whole dream from beginning to end was somehow—well—it was ὥσπερ αὔρα ἀπὸ χρηστῶν τόπων φέρουσα ὑγίειαν.[1]

'Don't tell Burrows, if you are seeing him. We all know what *he'd* make of a decapitation dream! As to yourself— as Humpty Dumpty said: "There's glory for you!"'

---

[1] Like a breeze blowing from excellent places, bearing health.

SELECTED WORKS BY OWEN BARFIELD